DIGITAL
BY
DESIGN

Hektor, Jürg Lehni

Spots, realities:united

Wavefunction,
Rafael Lozano-Hemmer

L.A.S.E.R. Tag, GRL

Home Movie 608-1,
Jim Campbell

PixelRoller,
rAndom international

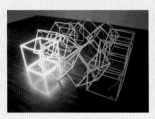

Moving Neon Cube, Jeppe Hein

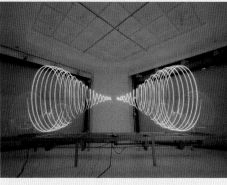

Palindrome, Conrad Shawcross

Tree,
Simon Heijdens

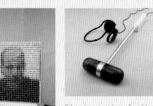

P*PHONE, Hulger

Planet Space Rover, Björn Schülke

Circles Mirror,
Daniel Rozin

Electroprobe, Troika

Risk Watch, Dunne & Raby

Peer Pressure Project,
Alice Wang

Laser Dress,
Hussein Chalayan

Volume, UVA

Lo-Rez-Dolores-Tabula-Rasa,
Ron Arad

Wooden Mirror,
Daniel Rozin

The Source,
Greyworld

ZXZX, Crispin Jones

DIGITAL BY DESIGN

Reed, Simon Heijdens

Desire Management,
Noam Toran

Furminator, fur

StreetWriter, IAA

Counter Void, Tatsuo Miyajima

Cloud, Troika

CRAFTING
TECHNOLOGY FOR
PRODUCTS AND
ENVIRONMENTS

Protrude, Flow,
Sachiko Kodama and
Minako Takeno

TROIKA /

Conny Freyer

Sebastien Noel

Eva Rucki

with 425 illustrations,
334 in colour

NeON,
Paul Cocksedge

Social Tele-Presence,
Auger-Loizeau

SHOWTIME, Julian Opie

Video Bulb,
Ryota Kuwakubo

Thames & Hudson

First published in the United Kingdom in 2008
by Thames & Hudson Ltd, 181A High Holborn,
London WC1V 7QX

First paperback edition 2010

Design: Conny Freyer and Eva Rucki, Troika

Design assistance: Grit Hartung

Text: Sebastien Noel, Troika

Typeset in Kraftek (designed by Troika), Deck
and Walbaum.

Jacket: Troika

British Library Cataloguing-in-Publication Data
A catalogue record for this book is available from
the British Library

ISBN 978-0-500-28901-3

Printed and bound in Hong Kong by Paramount
Printing Company Limited

To find out about all our publications, please visit
www.thamesandhudson.com. There you can subscribe
to our e-newsletter, browse or download our current
catalogue, and buy any titles that are in print.

Troika would like to thank all our contributors,
without whom this book wouldn't exist. Special
thanks go to Paola Antonelli, for her electric
enthusiasm and her amazing foreword, and to
Machiko Kusahara, Steven Sacks, Anthony Dunne,
Fiona Raby and Ron Arad, for sharing their
insights in the interviews. Additional thanks
go to Ron and Tony for their invaluable feedback
over the years, as well as for supporting this
project from a very early stage.

We would also like to express our gratitude
to Thames & Hudson's team: Lucas Dietrich, our
unfailingly supportive commissioning editor,
Cat Glover, for her assistance and patience,
and Ruby Quince, whose open-mindedness and
curiosity led to the commissioning of the book.

A special mention goes to the Arts Council, whose
grant enabled us to take the time to deepen our
research, and to the British Council for sending
us all over the world with their exhibitions,
giving us the opportunity to meet most of the
contributors in person.

Thanks to all of you who have helped us make this
book possible: Sabine Unamun at the Arts Council,
Emily Campbell and Nina Due at the British Council,
Noam Toran for his critical insights, Marcus Fairs
for his support and feedback, Hannah Redler from
the Science Museum, Ivan Poupyrev, Carsten and
Henry at Sony Research Lab in Tokyo, Anthony
Walker for the Japanese translations, Naoki Taichi
from Maywa Denki, Yuri Suzuki for opening doors
in Japan, and above all, our assistants, Emily
Hacker, Grit Hartung, Verena Hanschke and Vahakn
Matossian, for all their energy and hard work.

Last but not least, we would like to take the
opportunity to thank all the people who have
trusted and supported us over the four years of
our existence as Troika, above all, our friends
and families, as well as our mentors, forward-
thinking clients and all the people who shared
their professional expertise. Many thanks to Susie
Allen, Aoife, Laura and Demitra at Artwise Curators.

CONTENTS

3 / Guerrilla Artfare –
Disruption and
hardware hacking 140

FOREWORD
PAOLA ANTONELLI

Whether they use the skins and shells of objects as an interface or animate them from within, artists and designers are set on a path that will transform the world into an information parkour and enrich our lives with emotion and motion, direction, depth and freedom. It is a revolution that started several years ago, but technology – a wide word whose submenu for artists' consumption could read information, digital, nano-, bio-, and any other prefix that inspires a trip to the lab – is today available to a wider range of thinkers and doers, and sophisticated enough to be modulated with the lightness and precision of a laser (thirty years ago a hatchet would have done the trick). Artists and designers have also matured beyond the first moments of irrepressible and immoderate enthusiasm for the new mediums, and learned to control their touch and to wear technology, instead of letting technology wear them. To experience the works in this book – a highly distilled sample of today's best design and art production that uses technology in creative and unexpected ways – is to know how wonderful our present age can be.

Indeed, there is a touch of wide-eyed wonderment in every project, along with a friendly competitive feeling and the desire to share in the joy of discovery that is typical of communities of ninja-geek tinkerers who share unrequited passions. The great John Seely Brown, often considered one of the historical enablers of this technology transfer, calls it 'thinkering', to emphasize the high intellectual and innovative benefits that come from it. Indeed, in the hands of these brilliant artists, technology becomes a way to rediscover human nature, to push our most traditional buttons and also new ones we did not know we had, to make humans tick in a novel way. It sets us on the course of creation, collaboration, communication and construction that has become an impellent necessity and the only way to real future progress.

INTRODUCTION
TROIKA

From a crystal chandelier displaying SMS messages, electronic mirrors made of
wood to a tooth implant that allows for near-telepathic communication, the work
of a new generation of artists and designers rethinks technological innovation,
by exploring the potentials and impacts of new and creative technologies on an
aesthetic, formal, social and psychological level.

Whether mass products or experimental devices, immersive environments or custom-
made one-offs, these intricate pieces blur the boundaries between established
genres and disciplines, redefining both their contexts of use and modes of
distribution. They consistently avoid any attempt to categorize or label them,
the 'field' having been variously called new media art, digital art, techno design,
technocraft or physical computing, yet they are the imaginative products of
non-linear thinking, where technology is re-invested with subjectivity and play
and triggers thoughts just as a book or a film can do. These highly inspirational,
technology-infused works have started to grasp the collective imagination and
are already extensively relayed online. With hubs in the USA, Japan and Europe,
this movement is gaining momentum every day. The work of those artists and
designers is not only relevant in our increasingly technology-driven society
but can also shape the way we think, interact and engage with what is becoming
the dominant vehicle of cultural experience.

To try to understand the emergence of this movement, we need to outline briefly
the context in which it appears. At the end of the last millennium we saw the
transformation of the world into an information society, enabled by the digital
revolution, and whose cultural production is heavily mediated by and through
electronic technology. This has been associated with complex, far-reaching
paradigm shifts at the heart of society and culture, correlated with a dramatic
increase in speed and de-materialization into data. The impact of digital
technologies, with their capacity to deal with information and perform cognitive
functions while being interactive, is unprecedented. Consider, for instance, how
mobile telephony has changed our daily lives, the way we do business, interact
with our social networks or organize our time. Note the emergence of online
communities that freely share knowledge and information among people with
common interests, unlimited by geography. Observe the rise of internet dependency
syndrome. Technology is truly everywhere, its impact is profound and it mediates
our entire existence.

The digital society is also marked by immense paradoxes. It advocates freedom
but is control-obsessed, and comes complete with all the technological panoply
of machines and devices: CCTV, database, iris scan and ECHELON. It is a world that
strives by and for technology, and yet is consumed by technological nightmares,
fears of genetic modification, nanotechnological catastrophe or nuclear disaster.
On the one hand it is safer than ever, but on the other it is marked by bloody
conflicts and worldwide terror – which, too, has adopted mobile phones as the main
ignition technique for its bombs. The first world, moreover, enjoys a prosperous
economic climate and stability, which many suggest are the ideal conditions for
a cultural renaissance. Intense consumerism is the order of the day, entertained

Jürg Lehni
We Try Harder
2002

Cornel Windlin with Hektor for
the exhibition 'Public Affairs'
in the Kunsthaus Zurich

Max Dean, Raffaello D'Andrea,
Matt Donovan
Robotic Chair
1984–2006

by extreme political liberalism, bringing both first-class entrepreneurship and a flow or, more precisely, a flood of useless, redundant manufactured artefacts to sustain this frantic consumption. Cheap, bland and insipid, those ubiquitous artefacts represent perhaps the worst of material culture: über-functional gizmos, with in-built obsolescence and with more functions than you would ever need or dream of using, exist as a kind of uncanny misreading of the modernist credo. Quantity seems to be the only criteria that matters. Shortly before Christmas 2006, one of the world's biggest cargo ships, the Emma Maersk – dubbed SS Santa for the occasion – dumped on the coast of England over 45,000 tonnes of toys, mp3 players, phones and other gadgets from China.

The fact is that most of the objects that are supposed to satisfy our needs are not in tune with them any more. In a society such as ours, where all the basic needs are extensively met with a multitude of choice options, the multiplication of practical functions serves no real purpose. Instead, we have reached the upper levels of Maslow's hierarchy of needs where we seek more individual, psychological needs, such as self-fulfilment, self-affirmation and intellectual stimulation. This evolution represents a clear shift towards a more discerning consumer, often more affluent or at least better educated. The general lifestyle trend, evident in magazines but also apparent in the rise of more affordable, design-led brands, has contributed to this shift by diffusing and popularizing the culture of art and design. These phenomena are amplified by the rise of the new, influential Generation C, a generation not defined by age or background but by the desire to create, engage, debate and associate, and who flourished with the rise of the internet.

If art has always aimed to fulfil those higher needs, some design disciplines are already tapping into them, creating products with a character, which tell a story, arouse curiosity or stimulate our thoughts. The return of decoration in furniture design, as exemplified by Tord Boontje, is an excellent example of the return of humanism too into design, where magic, wonder and subjectivity represent a clear break with the minimal aesthetic and rational functionalism praised by modernism. Similar parallels can be drawn in architecture, fashion and most other fields of cultural creation, with the notable exception of technological artefacts. Technology is still largely developed in a linear, rational and scientific fashion, mostly for functional purposes and by global electronic corporations. This process, driven mainly by economic parameters and promoted by fine-tuned marketing, often relies on the inherent ability of software to introduce customization. Although this process can yield successful functional products, it has, with only a few rare exceptions, no real bearing on our higher psychological needs. Since technology is mediating our life, it is not too much to ask that it be meaningful and relevant. This is one of the arguments that motivate many of the artists and designers in this book.

This new generation of artists and designers, predominantly in their thirties, born amid the digital revolution speak the language of the machine like natives and understand technology intuitively, and these factors are fundamental to understanding the rise of technology-infused works, as they permit a natural, playful and more subjective development process. These artists were also born during the transition phase when analogue technologies were gradually replaced – the record players, the view-masters – and so they understand the benefits, appeal and importance of the materiality and tangibility of technologies compared with the all-digital and immaterial that prevailed at the start of the digital era.

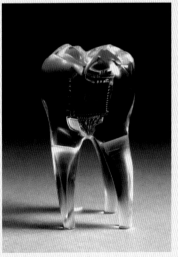

Auger–Loizeau
Audio Tooth Implant
2001–3

It is a generation that has also been greatly influenced by science fiction, by films such as Kubrick's 2001: A Space Odyssey and Scott's Blade Runner, novels such as Orwell's 1984 and Gibson's Neuromancer, Ballard's short stories and the hugely popular Star Wars, directed by George Lucas, to name but a few. The influence of sci-fi, in both its utopian and dystopian forms, helped build a common imagination, as well as sparking a willingness to think and create in technological terms, finding new avenues and alternative futures. This new wave of artists share, to a greater or lesser degree, an intense fascination with technology itself, its potential for artistic expression and its social and cultural impact. Other notable influences are to be found in kinetic and media art, the counterculture of the 1980s and 1990s – more precisely in DJ culture, which influenced the process in terms of remixing, hacker communities, as in the Berlin-based Chaos Computer Club, street art and graffiti.

Highly educated, this cross-fertilized generation has assimilated the teachings of post-modernism: the protagonists share an irreverent outlook on the impasse of modernism and a preference for a more subjective approach, while often borrowing post-modern processes – namely the re-appropriation, the re-use and the ready-made, the mixing of genres. Yet, fundamental factors separate them from post-modernists: they often have a positive, engaged outlook on life and its meaning, and strive to create a novel language and genuine works. They engage too in constant exchange and debate, sharing knowledge in online communities and adhering to an open-source philosophy often associated with a critical approach. Their process is flexible and associative, pulling together the right competences while sometimes venturing into unorthodox collaborations, as have artist Ben Rubin and statistics expert Marc Hansen for Listening Post (p. 86). This phenomenon is visible in the number of collectives represented in this book.

These artists and designers seek, in their practice, beauty, depth, relevance and meaning, often acting in reaction to the standard aesthetic and form and the status quo. They engage with technology to reveal its intrinsic beauty and find its true language, treating it as a tool for discovering new forms or as a raw, upgraded material with which to create their designs. Take, for example, the computer-grown chairs of Laarman (p. 24), the mechanical dresses of Chalayan (p. 28) or Geoffrey Mann's (p. 46) Flight series, where he uses a combination of cinematographic techniques, CAD and rapid prototyping to create the physical traces described by a bird at take-off, thereby materializing time. Another approach is exploring the interactivity and the possibilities opened up by multimedia and electronics to create immersive experiences and installations rich in emotions and narrative, theatricality and magic. The examples are many, both in the design and in the fine art field, and this book features among others the work of Simon Heijdens (p. 60), with his interactive projection of trees that respond to outside winds, or the fantastic installations of Lozano-Hemmer (p. 90), McIntosh (p. 104) and Kodama (p. 124).

These creators also explore the area where analogue and digital intersect, bringing feeling and warmth to an otherwise cold and immaterial construct. This is perhaps most brilliantly represented by the non-reflective mirror series of Daniel Rozin (p. 82), but is a common denominator for many of the protagonists of this book. Acting more in guerrilla mode, they use and abuse technology to forge humourous weapons for disrupting the established order or to re-appropriate commercial devices into meaningful, surprising experiences. Theirs is a proactive attitude in a world of bafflingly apathetic quietism. From the Institute of Applied Autonomy's guerrilla printing machines (p. 142) to Altman's micro device that turns off all the surrounding TVs (p. 152), from the hardware-remixed objects of Ibars (p. 190) to the hack scanners turned photographic camera of Golembewski (p. 170), this irreverent approach is rich in results and consequences. The book also showcases examples of inventions that have gone beyond the prototype stage to engage with the world of consumerism. They are mass-produced and distributed as artistic devices and, stemming as they do from a reaction to the bluntness of commercial electronics, they reach audiences away from the art galleries. Among the best-known examples are Hulger (p. 196), with their beautifully quirky handsets, and many Japanese artists, whose work forms a sub-movement called device art – see for instance Kuwakubo's art gadgets (p. 212). In opposition to today's rampant individualism, the creations are often meant to be shared, enjoyed collectively and to develop platforms for change and exchange, as in the installation of Usman Haque (p. 64) or the sumptuous public displays by realities:united (p. 70). Some of these new artists and designers also engage in a critical discourse to explore the social and psychological impacts of technology and invent artefacts and experiences that connect with the real, complicated pleasures and states of the human mind often neglected by conventional design or alternatives to the current technologies, loaded with hope and intelligence. The strange products of

Hulger
P*PHONE
2003

Dunne & Raby (p. 234), Noam Toran (p. 224) or the disturbing installations
of Marie Sester (p. 222) are but a few examples featured here.

We wanted Digital By Design to be a testimony to the effervescent energy of
this field. We hope the book will entertain, inspire, arouse curiosity and contribute
to the debate about the role and forms of these technologies, which are mainly
intended here as interactive and digital — including rapid prototyping and
manufacturing — electronics and mechatronics.

Beyond the technologies themselves, the attitudes and motivations of the artists
and designers featured, their search for meaning, quality and personal investment
in a world that struggles to provide it, perhaps represent a broader societal
phenomenon and the aspirations of the new generation, who, we hope, will contribute
many great works in the years to come.

Troika.

Maywa Denki, Ryota Kuwakubo
Bitman
2004
© Yoshimoto Kogyo Co. Ltd

[left]
Dunne & Raby
Technological Dream Series:
No. 1, Robots
2007

Robot No. 4

1/DESIGN NOUVEAU
DIGITAL FORMS
AND ELECTRIC
BEAUTY

Design Nouveau presents works that explore the aesthetic potential
of technology, skilfully revealing its intrinsic beauty in an alliance
between form, process and concept. The artists and designers here
exhibit a variety of approaches, using technology either as a tool for
discovering and creating new forms or as a raw material, which they
transform in spectacular ways and integrate into their creations.
Always, these approaches go beyond the realm of mere possibilities
and technical prowess, and the examples in this chapter demonstrate
their potential, adapting and incorporating new and old technologies
to create truly new and fascinating objects and revealing technology's
true language, physical qualities and stunning beauty.

PANDORA FREDRIKSON STALLARD

SHAPE-SHIFTING
CHANDELIER

Leading figures of British avant-garde design
Fredrikson Stallard believe that the imperatives
of modernism – mass production and the prevalence
of a rational and functional approach – are now
obsolete. Instead, their pieces are intended as
sophisticated fairytales for grown-ups. They speak
to the mind in subliminal narratives, and instil
controversial feelings of opulence, decay and
fragility. The sensual darkness of their work opens
the doors of a mysterious and fantastic world, where
their designs become the protagonists in our own
imaginary piece of theatre.

With Pandora, Fredrikson Stallard have developed a
piece whose form is never permanent but constantly
destroyed and recreated through movement. Starting
from a traditional chandelier arrangement, the 1,990
crystals slowly move apart, recreating a motion of
explosion, before slowly coming back together to
their original form. Here, the motion brings the
reflection of the crystals to life, while the continuous
explosion–implosion of the chandelier creates a
theatrical relationship between the piece and the
viewer, as it leaves the conventional spatial territory
of the chandelier and enters our own level. With
Pandora, Fredrikson Stallard use technology as an
illusionist might use it: to enable the magic and allow
for the poetry and theatrical dimensions of the piece
to emerge. Yet it is nowhere to be seen.

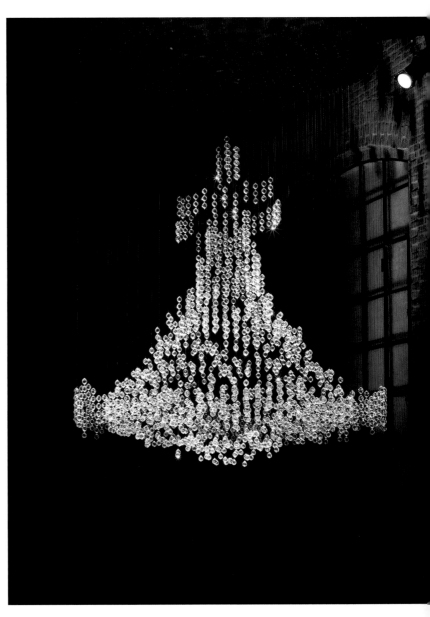

Pandora
for Swarovski Crystal Palace Collection
2007

NEON
GAS-FILLED LIGHT PENDANTS

CRYSTALLIZE LASER CHANDELIER

PAUL COCKSEDGE

In his work, Paul celebrates the magical qualities of lights, creating technically ingenious pieces with stunning visual appeal. His 2003 NeON is a beguiling example of the designer's ability to reveal the intrinsic beauty of technology. A cluster of light pendants, NeOn is made of hand-blown glass vessels that have been filled with neon gas and that glow with a subtle red light when an electrical current is passed through them. The principle is similar to conventional neon tubes used in advertising signs, but the larger diameter of the phials produces a softer, more enigmatic glow. The form of the vessels, reminiscent of some alchemist's instrumentation, further accentuates the ethereal appeal of the lights. With NeON, Paul Cocksedge manages to turn a standard technology into a poetic and subtle light sculpture, which carries the magic of early Victorian scientific apparatus. It reminds us of the work of Johann Geissler (1815–79), early inventor of the neon tube and famous for his quirkily beautiful and elaborate glowing glass tubes.

Another stunning example is his Crystallize chandelier, in which lasers have been chosen for their intense and vibrant light, while literally 'drawing with the light'. Designed for Swarovski's Crystal Palace Collection and presented in Milan in 2005, Crystallize features two 3mW green laser modules hung at the bottom of a frame, which create beams that are reflected by four tiny mirrors, thus tracing the iconic Swarovski crystal shape in the air. A real crystal is suspended in the middle of the frame, creating magical sparkles and reflections as it diffracts the laser light. Here, technology is used for its aesthetic and dramatic impact, and incorporated into the design pretty much as a raw material, albeit with great and effortless artistry.

NeON
2003

Glass vessels filled with gas
10 x 10 x 50 cm (4 x 4 x 20 in.)
(each vessel)

Crystallize
for Swarovski Crystal Palace Collection
2005

Crystals, laser module and glass
Height ranges from 90 to 180 cm
(35 to 71 in.)

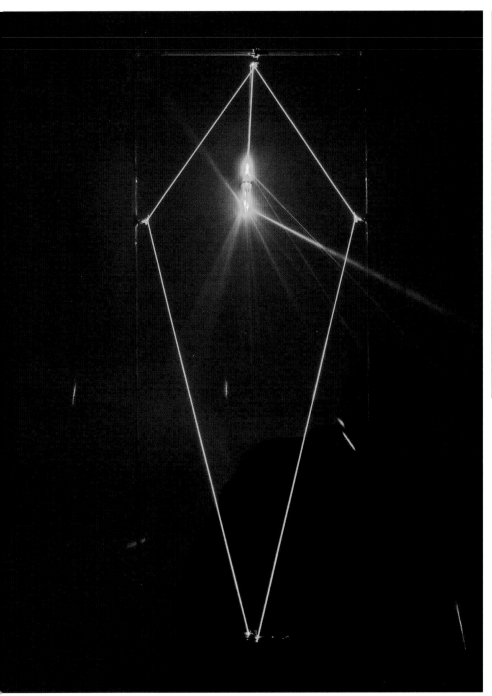

BONE FURNITURE
JORIS LAARMAN

FURNITURE MIMICKING
NATURAL GROWTH

What if the computer became the designer? What if, instead of using digital technology to create a vision that we have, we taught the machine how to design, to set some starting parameters, evaluate the results and select the most appropriate, appealing ones? With the help of car manufacturer Opel, Joris Laarman created an algorithm that mimics the way trees and bones naturally grow. Trees have the ability to add material where it is needed, whereas bones will take out matter where it is structurally superfluous. Starting from an original on-screen blob of material, and setting the growth parameters and the forces applied on the chair, the software grows a series of chairs and chaises that are not only structurally optimized – as the material is placed only where it is needed – but also shares the intricate lightness and irregular complexity of natural shapes. Laarman subsequently went on to materialize the most successful results. The Bone Chair shown here is cast in aluminium; the Bone Chaise is made of a translucent polyurethane resin. Far from imposing style arbitrarily on matter, Laarman demonstrates an original, alternative use of artificial intelligence.

Bone Chaise
2007

Shore 90 crystal clear UV-resistant
polyurethane resin

For gallery Friedman Benda, New York
& droog

[above and opposite top]
in progress

[opposite bottom]
Cast

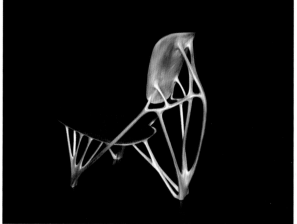

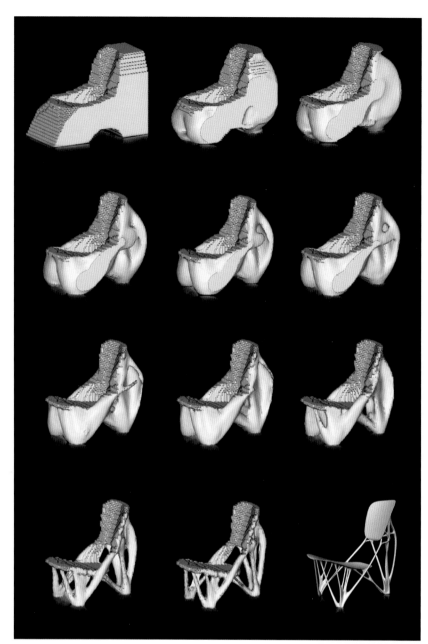

[above]
Bone Chair
2007

Seat & back rest: highly polished aluminium
Struts: silk polished aluminium

For gallery Barry Friedman Ltd, New York,
& droog

[left]
Bone Chair, optimization

[bottom]
Bone Chair cast, rendering

[opposite]
Bone Chair polished

«IN A WAY [THE SOFTWARE] QUITE PRECISELY COPIES
THE WAY EVOLUTION CONSTRUCTS. I DIDN'T USE IT TO
CREATE THE NEXT WORLD'S PERFECT CHAIR BUT AS
A HIGH TECH SCULPTING TOOL TO CREATE ELEGANT
SHAPE WITH A KIND OF LEGITIMACY.» JORIS LAARMAN

MECHANICAL DRESSES
TRANSFORMING DRESSES

LASER DRESSES
LASER-
ENHANCED
GARMENTS

HUSSEIN CHALAYAN

Hussein Chalayan is one of the most innovative and experimental fashion designers of this time. From his graduate collection, which looked at the aesthetic of decomposition and featured silk garments covered with iron filings, buried and exhumed, the work of Chalayan is stamped by a preference for the process over the final result, a conceptual approach that contrasts sharply with that of his contemporaries and which reflects his more artistic influences. His seminal 2000 collection, a spectacularly staged and much acclaimed event, featured a range of table and chairs that mechanically transformed into clothing and accessories, the round coffee table into a long, slinky, wooden dress, the chairs into suitcases. The theme of the collection, infused with Chalayan's Cypriot background, was how to conceal and wear possessions in wartime.

Chalayan further explored the potential of mechanical transformation in a different context: for his 'One Hundred and Eleven' spring/summer 2007 collection, he retraced the history of over a century of fashion by creating six Mechanical Dresses that morph from one iconic silhouette of a decade to another. Embedded in the dresses is a series of micro-motors and smart wires, which enable the dresses to change cut, fabric to be pulled or dropped, the waist to enlarge and zippers to open and close. At a time when smart fabrics and wearable computing remain buzz-words in the textile world, Chalayan's Mechanical Dresses use technology to demonstrate a poignant vision of what the future of fashion could be: sensual, poetic and intellectually stimulating. Later collections feature a video dress with hundreds of integrating LEDs, or a neo-scifi automated veil, which closes like a cocoon around the model's head. It is a vision of fashion that, says Chalayan, 'fills the gap between fantasy and reality'.

[above]
The Morphing Hood Coat
Autumn/winter 2007

Womenswear Collection: Airborne

[opposite]
Laser Dresses
Spring/summer 2008

Womenswear Collection: Readings

[overleaf]
Mechanical Dress – 1940s–1960s
Spring/summer 2007

Womenswear Collection: One Hundred
and Eleven

LOLITA
SMS MESSAGES
CHANDELIER

LO-REZ-DOLORES-
TABULA-RASA
FIBRE OPTIC
VIDEO WALL

RON ARAD

One of the most influential figures of contemporary design, Ron Arad has, since the early 1980s, consistently managed to escape categorization, subverting the boundaries between genres and disciplines with his trademark approach: irreverent, innovative, ingenious and highly experimental. In his many fields of practice, architecture, furniture, interiors, products, public art, one-off and limited-edition studio pieces, he is recognized for his radical, uncompromising and progressive attitude, which has enabled him to remain at the cutting edge of design.

Among the first designers to explore the possibilities of interactivity, electronics and other digital technologies, with which he tinkered back in the mid-1980s, Arad recently created the two pieces featured here, his 2004 chandelier Lolita, created for Swarovski, and the large installation Lo-Rez-Dolores-Tabula-Rasa. Lolita consists of 2,100 crystals, illuminated from within by 1,050 high-powered LEDs, arranged to form a spiralling ribbon hanging from the ceiling. The chandelier acts as a pixel-board to display text messages sent via SMS. The clever interplay between the function of the chandelier, the fact that the messages are always visible, thanks to its omni-directional spiralling shape, and the context of its interaction scenario – as it is generally displayed for design events, in high-end clubs and at socialites' parties – makes Lolita a highly successful and iconic piece of technologically enhanced design.

The same year, Arad created one of his most ambitious technological pieces to date, an installation made in collaboration with Corian™ Dupont featuring an 8 x 4-metre (26 x 13-foot) white synthetic marble wall embedded with over 27,000 individual fibre optic strands capable of 'injecting' light into a slate of the translucent material and magically transforming the smooth surface of the wall into a low-resolution, full-colour display. Contrasting with the blackness of other display technologies, Lo-Rez-Dolores-Tabula-Rasa presents a uniform white surface when switched off, while displaying a unique, intriguing aesthetic of the image when turned on. As the fibres terminate just below the surface of the material, the light they bring diffuses according to its intensity. As a result,

Lolita
for Swarovski Crystal Palace Collection
Milan, Italy, 2004

2,100 crystals, 1,050 white LEDs
embedded in the crystal, 1 km of
nine-ways cable-braided shielding
and 31 processors
15.4 x 9.5 x 8.6 cm
(61 x 37 x 34 in.)

each pixel on the wall – corresponding to each of
the fibres – appears to grow in size and contract
according to the film displayed. But beside the unique
analogue qualities of the display itself lies another,
equally fascinating world: the back of the wall. There
the 27,000 fibres gather to create ever-growing strands
as they reach the central optical device responsible
for sending the light information of the film into each
individual light conduit. It feels like being in the brain
of a fantastic living organism, as each strand of 550
kilometres (342 miles) of fibre optic starts to glow
over its length with the colour of its representative
pixel, creating an ever-evolving light sculpture. Here,
the colourful, extraneous vision of technology Arad
has developed over his career expands to its fullest,
creating a magnificent, mesmerizing experience.
Along with the wall, a pill-shaped table embedded
with 20,000 fibres demonstrated the versatility
of the technique applied here on a non-flat surface.

Lo-Rez-Dolores-Tabula-Rasa
IX Biennale di Architettura, Italian
Pavilion, Giardini della Biennale,
Venice, Italy, 2004

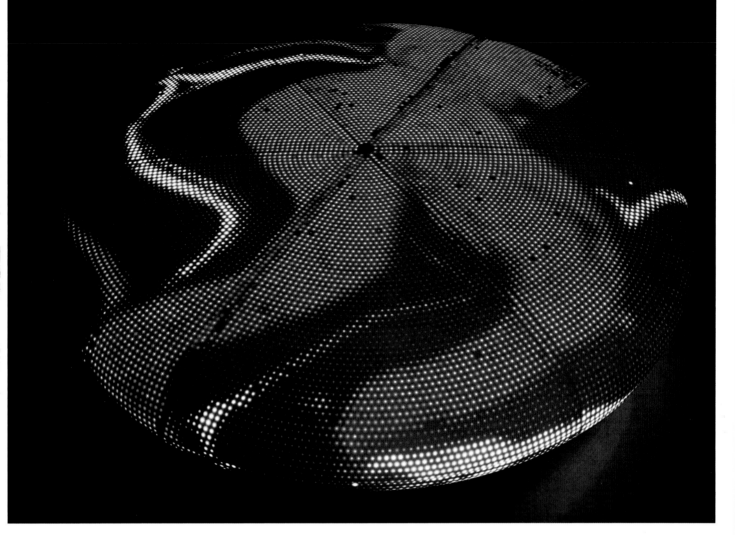

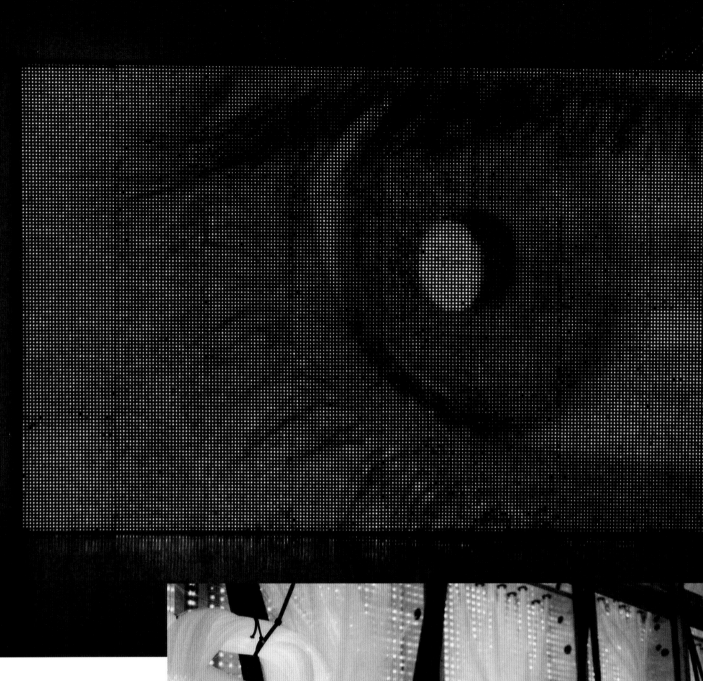

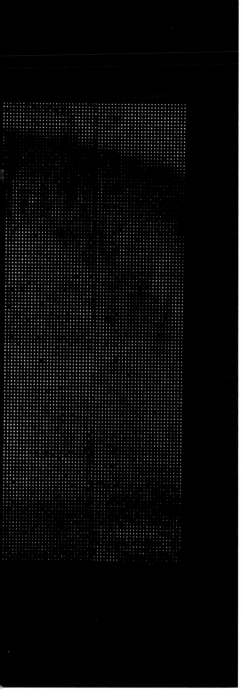

«IT WAS IMPORTANT WHEN
PLANNING THIS INSTALLATION
NOT TO DWELL ON THE
TECHNICAL – 'HOW DOES IT
WORK' – SIDE OF THINGS.
MORE THAN THAT, WE TOOK
A LOT OF CARE NOT TO REVEAL
HOW IT WAS DONE, KNOWING
FULL WELL THAT THE BACK
OF THE WALL COULD POSSIBLY
BE JUST AS EXCITING AS THE
FRONT. OUR ANXIETY WAS
FOCUSED ON THE FRONT AND
MORE ON THE 'WILL IT WORK'
RATHER THAN 'HOW DOES IT
WORK'. IT DID – BEAUTIFULLY!»
RON ARAD

[opposite top]
Lo-Rez-Dolores

IX Biennale di Architettura, Italian
Pavilion, Giardini della Biennale,
Venice, Italy, 2004

[above and opposite bottom]
Lo-Rez-Dolores
back

CLONE CHAISE
SURFACE INTELLIGENT OBJECT

SAM BUXTON

Sam Buxton's work crosses perceived boundaries
between art, design and science, innovatively using
advanced material and technologies. Best known for
his hugely successful series of Mikro laser-etched,
miniature fold-up sculptures, he pioneered the use
of printed electroluminescent displays to create
vernacular objects whose surface can communicate,
display information and react to its user. These
explorations form part of a series called SIOs –
surface intelligent objects – and includes the Clone
Chaise, which graphically maps the systems of the
human body. When this object is approached, the
heart begins to beat and the lungs appear to breathe.
Buxton's work seeks more intimately to integrate
information displays in ordinary objects by exploiting
properties inherent to electroluminescent technology
displays – they are thin, bendy and shockproof.

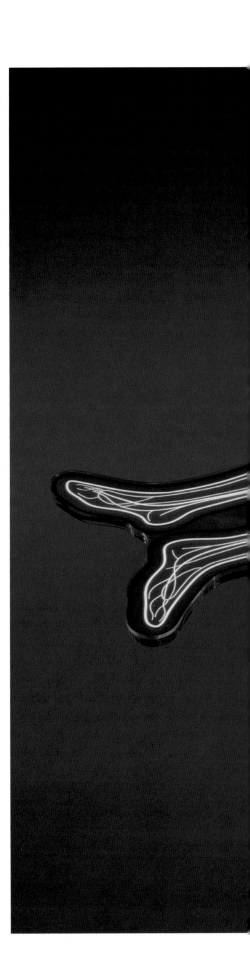

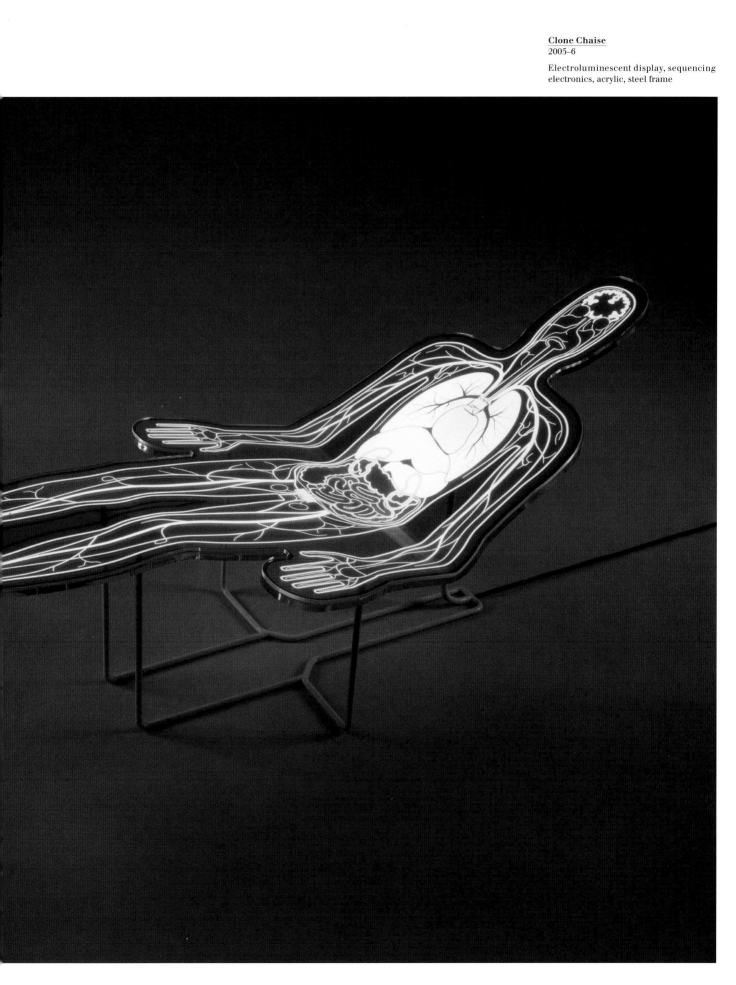

ARCHEOLOGY OF THE FUTURE
STIJN OSSEVOORT

INTELLIGENT BOOK COVER

With advances in miniaturization and printed electronics, components are now small enough to install electronic behaviour in any object. Often, though, electronics is added to the product as a mere extra layer. In his book Archeology of the Future, an anthology of essays about visions of the future in the areas of science and technology, Ossevoort sought a more intimate integration between the electronics and the object, in terms of both functionality and meaning and of the technology itself. The book, released as a limited edition of 150, integrates in its cover a series of printed heating elements, which change the colour of the thermo-chromic ink used, revealing a series of words and symbols, as the ink changes from black to blue. Several motion sensors as well as a microphone enable a small microchip in the spine to detect how the book is being handled, and control the symbols to be revealed and their sequence accordingly. The microchip also memorizes sequences of events to shape the behaviour of the book in future. As such, the book becomes a kind of oracle, generating responses in the form of an enigmatic statement or allegory, a concept well suited to the content of the book itself.

Archeology of the Future
2007

Design & Production: Stijn Ossevoort
Graphic Design: Jonas Voegeli
Programming: Jamie Ward

REICH

ANFANGEN

JETZT

WIR O CHLOROPHYLL VOR
HÖLLE WASSER REBELLEN BEGEG-
NUNG VON RECHNEN DARAUS
SOGAR LEHREN EINTRETEN GEMISCH
NATÜRLICH MAXIMAL FAHREN
WERT DERSELBE WIEDER DESHALB KOMPASS WIRD KÖRPER GIBT WIR
MASSE ZURÜCK HART Y SCHRITT HABE BILDER KLEIN HERAUS
HEISS STELLEN VORSTELLUNGEN SICH INNERHALB DAUER DENKEN IM
VERHÄLTNIS ACHT GOLD MÄSSIG ZEIT UNTEN GEGEN ALS FÜR

ZWEI | ASCHE | FOLGT | EIN MAL
| SPIEGEL | ICH | ? | ROT |
MACHEN | WINTER | STATT | REICH | Σ | JA
| GESTERN | BRÜCKE | NACHT | 9 |
SICHER | □ | PFEFFER | HERZ | ← | SCHEINT
| NETZEN | ENDE | ! | LABYRINTH |
WARM | % | 8 | JETZT | MORGEN | WELT
| RAUM | BEGEGNET | ∴ | ALLE |
GARTEN | OK | ⊂ | WIRD | MEER | DUNKEL
| NO | AH | LEBEN | ⌐ | X | VIEL | HEIL |
ZAHL | ANFANGEN | ∅ | SEIN
| ÜBERMORGEN | MILLIONEN | HAUS |
LICHT | DU | ELF | IMMER | MOND
| Δ |

BALD QUER FASSEN § NATÜRLICH MAN SEHR UNWAHR-
SCHEINLICH BEFINDEN IN PLÖTZLICH DASSELBE AN-
FANGS GEHEN WAHRSCHEINLICH ENTFERNEN ALSO EI-
NES P ZUSTAND SCHLUSS MÜSSEN 207 DIE 1. ABNEHMEN
NICHT A KRIEG PHYSIKALISCH 799 DER SPEZIELL DAGE-
GEN MACHEN DAS GANZE SYSTEM ABGETRENNT
ABER GLEICH 2 KANN OBJEKT ZERSTÖRT DIES WENN SO
AN AUCH UM EINZIG UNSER UNGLEICH CHALLANGE
MOLEKÜLE WELCHE BESTIMMT EINSAM ODYSSEE BEWE-
GUNG ERDE VON BEOBACHTUNG ERWARTEN AUF VIEL
DASS ANNAHME ZU IST NACH UNS ERFAHRUNGEN BIS
DENN 3 DÜRFTE IN FAHRT ISOLIERT METHODE HAUPT
SPÄTER SICH SATZ SCHLIESSLICH SEIN ZU HALTEN EIN-
FACH SPEKULATION NACH MECHANISCH WIRKLICH GE-
WISS WÄRME LEITUNG UNIVERSUM GRUND C SCHEINT
BILD BESONDERS HATTE STAND WUNDER BOLTZMANN
ZUGLEICH WAR LUFT AN LEBEN MUSS QUARZ SCHWEIN
PHYSIK GESCHAFFEN BLEIBEN JAHRE WEIT AUS NACH-
DEM MACH 21 IDEE IST UND DAVON IRGEND GESTEHEN
PERSÖNLICHKEIT ANALYSE ÜBER TOD FORSCHUNG PRO-

GRAMM VERTEIDIGEN IRR FEST JUNG HYPOTHESE ALLE
BEIN ALS SCHLACHT BEDEUTUNG THEORIE BAR FALSCH
GANG KÜHN ÜBERZEUGEND SINNE FOLGEN UNGEORD-
NET ZUNEHMEN FORM BEWEIS VERKNÜPFT GLAUBE STA-
TISTISCH DATUM SYMMETRISCH NUN HÄUFIG JE WENIG-
WEICH UNGEORDNUNG ZUKUNFT GAR EINWAND BEOBACH-
TE FÜHRT ZUNÄCHST KEINE GENAU WIEDER RICHTUNG
GEBIETE SELTEN NEHMEN NENNEN EINZEL WELT SUK-
ZESS GELTEN BEWUSSTSEIN TIER GESETZ PFEIL SCHNITT
LAND FLUKTUATION WELTEN DENEN SCHLAGEN FOL-
GENDE WINZIG HIRN DIMENSIONEN WEICHEN BEIDE
WITZ MITTELPUNKT BENENNUNG OHNE ATEM RAUB
MACHT FINDEN SELBER WIDERSPRUCH ANTI WACHSTUM
VERSUCH ≈ 10 STELLT BEHAUPTE KOLLISIONEN HÄLFTE
BEHÄLTER PRAKTISCH HEISST INTERPRETATION SIEHE
SYSTEME ANDERES KONSTRUKTIVITÄT FOLGLICH GÜLTIG
TROTZDEM MEINER 382 SEITE SINCE OF AUSSFRECHEN
DAMIT VERTEIDIGEN BRINGEN VERGEBLICH DEPRESSION
AD WAR JEGLICHE BLIEB GEHÖREN SUBJEKTIV SUBJEKTI-
VISMUS HOFFEN ZWISCHEN LANG DAUERND JAHRHUN-

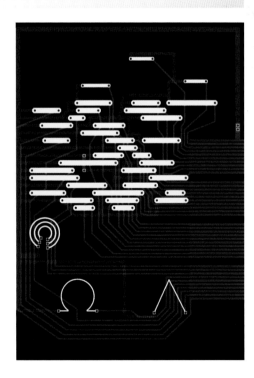

PEGASUS AND THE WINGED LION ETCH SERIES CHRISTOPHER PEARSON

VIRTUAL RELIEFS

3D ENGRAVED ORNAMENTS

Christopher Pearson is interested in the idea of digital craftsmanship. He believes that digital design often lacks the quality of execution of a skill-based approach traditionally associated with craft, where a master would thoroughly understand every aspect of his art. Pearson is best known for his animated projected wallpapers – technologically upgraded versions of traditional wallpaper designs, in which the patterns move to follow rich narratives and carefully timed animations – but it is possibly with one of his latest projects, large, laser-etched glass panels created for British Airways' new Terminal 5 lounges in Heathrow Airport, that his idea of digital craft finds itself fully expressed. The concept of digital craftsmanship goes hand in hand with attempts to turn abstract digital technologies into compelling and tangible objects, exploring their material implications in an attempt to find their natural language. Here, Pearson explores a relatively new technique called 3D laser-etching – usually employed to create miniature tri-dimensional pictures into blocks of glass as souvenirs – and turns it into one of the most delicate and beautiful digital tools used so far. By forming 3D patterns within the volume of thick panels of glass, Pearson twists the traditional repeating wallpaper patterns and introduces a third dimension: the patterns now really flow in space instead of being mere trompe-l'oeil. The ethereal materiality of those crystalline leaves and flowers is subtly reinforced by lighting along the edge of the glass panels.

In another project commissioned for the British Airways lounges, Pegasus and the Winged Lion, Pearson has produced a kind of animated relief. Cleverly using shadows and highlights, he creates an animated trompe l'oeil by suddenly morphing the stone brickwork and bringing to life the traditional and time-honoured British Airways crest, animating its two characters, Pegasus and the Winged Lion, in a series of humorous sequences. Here too, the idea of digital craftsmanship is central to the piece.

[above]
Oak Seasons
2007

5 pairs of 3D laser-etched glass screens
From the Etch Series
3 x 1.4 m (9 ft 10 in. x 4 ft 7 in.) each
British Airways Concorde Galleries
Lounge, Terminal 5, Heathrow, London

[opposite and left]
Pegasus and the Winged Lion
2008

Digitally animated trompe l'oeil
stone carving
From the Digital Relief Series
1.5 x 1.8 m (4 ft 11 in. x 5 ft 11 in.)
British Airways Concorde Galleries
Lounge, Terminal 5, Heathrow, London

BOOK OF LIGHTS POP-UP LUMINAIRE
TAKESHI ISHIGURO

Remember the pop-up books of your childhood, the anticipation and surprise that came with them, as you unfolded paper monsters and castles at every page? With Book of Lights, Ishiguro revives this excitement, albeit in a slightly upgraded format. The ordinary-looking coffee-table book opens up into a classic lamp design, illuminated by integrated LEDs, becoming a poetic, innocent source of light. The remarkable sensibility of this design is typical of Ishiguro, who works from his studio/laboratory in Tokyo on a wide range of projects, from mass-produced products to installations. Ishiguro is noteworthy for his experimental approach and his use of unconventional materials, such as smoke. In his 2002 installation at the International House of Japan in Roppongi, he created a machine that expels giant smoke rings into the air above the garden. Another example is his mesmerizing mercury fountain, a prototype that uses mercury in place of water.

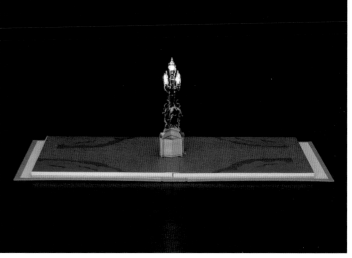

Book of Lights
2007

Published and produced by Artechnica

FLIGHT ATTRACTED TO LIGHT GEOFFREY MANN

**ETIENNE-JULES MAREY
IN THE 21ST CENTURY**

**STEREOLITHOGRAPHY CHANDELIER
TRACING A MOTH'S MOVEMENTS**

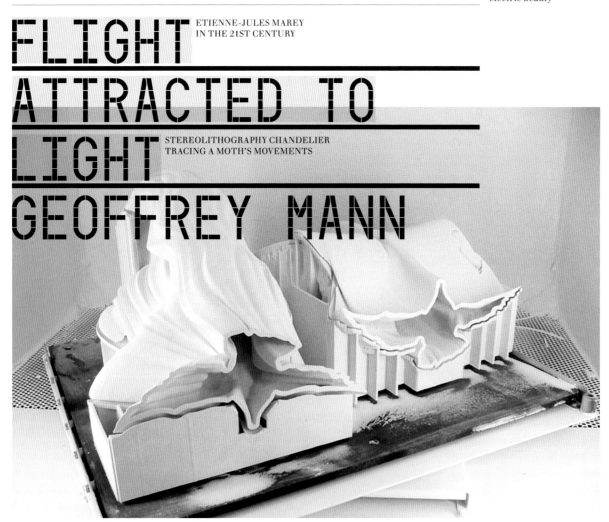

Geoffrey Mann describes himself as a product artist.
His work explores the possibilities and impacts
on the physical form of digital media and digital
manufacturing. Reminiscent of the work of Etienne-
Jules Marey, both Attracted to Light and Flight
materialize the motion of animals through space
and time. Part of a series appropriately called Long
Exposure, Attracted to Light depicts in a solid object
the shape created by the erratic movements of a moth
flying around a light bulb over a short time. Using a
combination of cinematic techniques, CAD modelling
and rapid prototyping, the object encapsulates the
sheer natural beauty of the moth's flight, while
demonstrating a novel aesthetic. Mann reiterates
this process with Flight, this time materializing the
movements of a bird landing and taking off. The final
objects are either presented as rapid-prototypes or
later cast in glass.

[above]
Flight
2006
in progress

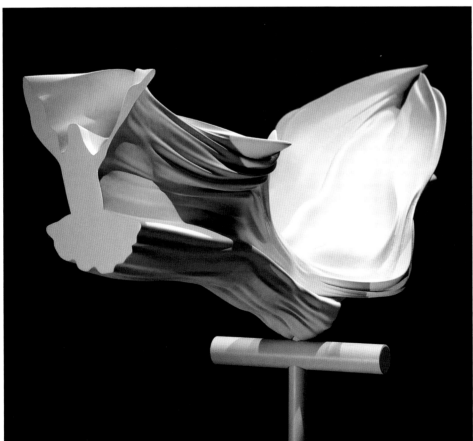

[above]
Attracted to Light, Moth
Long Exposure series
2005

Rapid-prototype, FDM
250 x 300 x 35 cm (98 x 118 x 14 in.)

[left]
Flight, Landing
Long Exposure series
2006

Rapid-prototype, Z-corp
65 x 35 x 45 cm (25 x 14 x 18 in.)

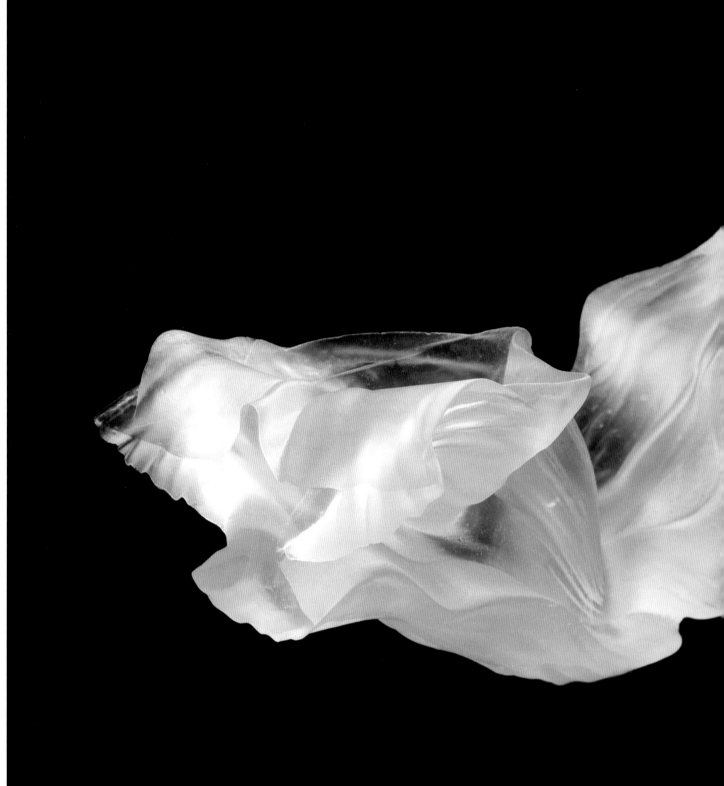

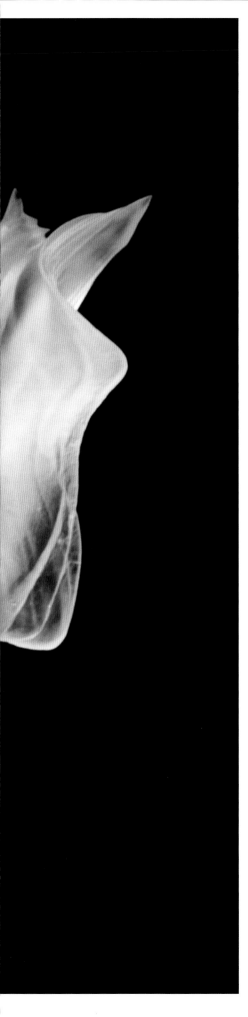

Flight, Landing
Long Exposure series
2005

Kiln cast glass
65 x 35 x 45 cm
(25 x 14 x 18 in.)

CHANGING
CUPBOARD
CHANGING SIGNBOARD
CUPBOARD
SKETCH
FURNITURE
MOTION-CAPTURE FURNITURE
FRONT

With <u>Sketch Furniture</u>, Swedish design group Front have developed a method of 3D motion-capture technology to materialize freehand sketches executed in air. Pen strokes made in the air are recorded to become 3D digital files in real time. These are then post-treated and materialized by means of rapid-prototyping, into real physical pieces. This system opens up several further interesting possibilities. It represents such a simplification of the highly skilled CAD process usually employed to create 3D models that it is likely almost anyone could use it without previous knowledge. The technique brings a performance element to 3D modelling, as well as providing it with the character, spontaneity and speed of drawing.

Another of Front's notable ventures into technology is their <u>Changing Cupboard</u>, one of the few examples of electronic technology directly embedded into furniture. The surfaces of a freestanding cupboard are built out of turning advertising signs so that the graphics covering the cupboard change periodically. This item is part of their Found collection, in which the designers changed existing objects and parts into novel artefacts.

Changing Cupboard
Stockholm, 2007

«MOTION CAPTURE IS A TECHNIQUE THAT TRANSLATES MOTIONS INTO 3D FILES. MOTION CAPTURE IS MOSTLY USED FOR ANIMATIONS IN MOVIES AND COMPUTER GAMES. WE HAVE USED THE TECHNIQUE TO SIMPLY RECORD THE TIP OF A PEN WHEN WE DRAW PIECES OF FURNITURE IN THE AIR.» FRONT

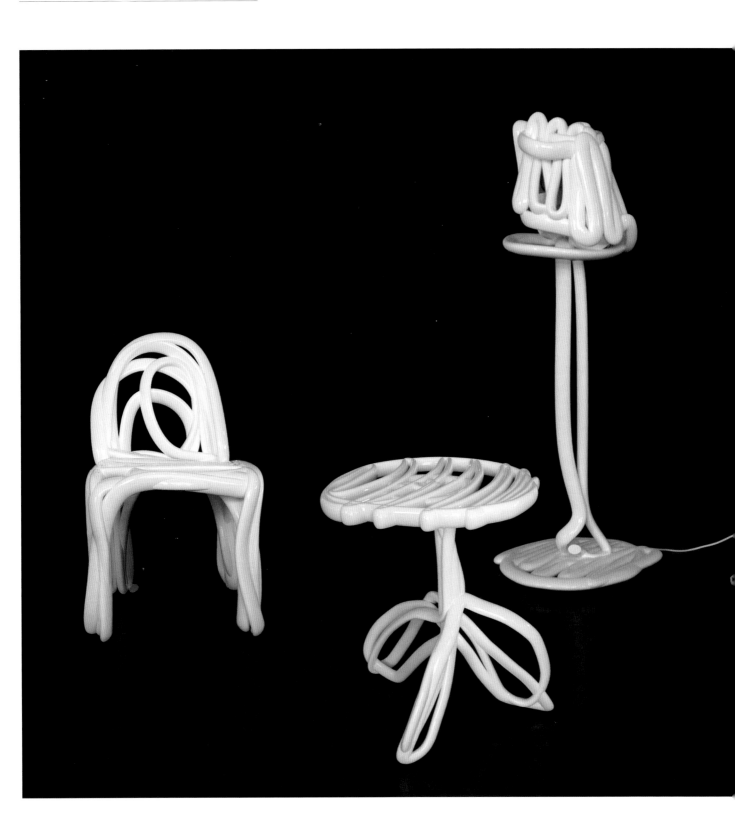

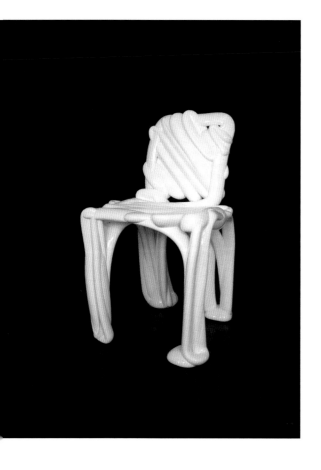

Sketch Furniture
Art Basel Miami, Design 2005
with Barry Friedman Gallery Ltd,
New York

PONG TABLE
ARCADE GAME
HIDDEN IN A TABLE
BY ROYAL
APPOINTMENT
CHAMELEON CHAIRS
MORITZ
WALDEMEYER

Moritz Waldemeyer is a mechatronics expert and technical wizard and the man the design pundits call in when they need their wildest technological dreams to come to life. Moritz programmed Ron Arad's Lolita chandelier, helped design the systems behind Hussein Chalayan's series of mechanical dresses and put together his video dress, and engineered Fredrikson Stallard's Pandora chandelier, to mention but a few of the projects he has been involved in.

He also designed pieces of his own, such as the Pong Table, featured here, a table made of white Corian with 2,500 LEDs integrated below its top. When switched on, the practical dining table surface vanishes and the LEDs shine through the material to display the classic video game Pong. The interface is integrated in the table as two small track pads on each end. Another piece, By Royal Appointment,

shows a series of tall black chairs with integrated multicoloured LED backlighting. A sensor in the backrest detects the colour worn by someone sitting on the chair and adjusts the backlighting to provide a kind of colour-coordinated aura.

Moritz is of particular interest, as he enables people with highly creative minds but who may lack the required skills to realize their visions, as the stunning pieces conceived by Arad or Chalayan demonstrate with their powerful and alternative visions.

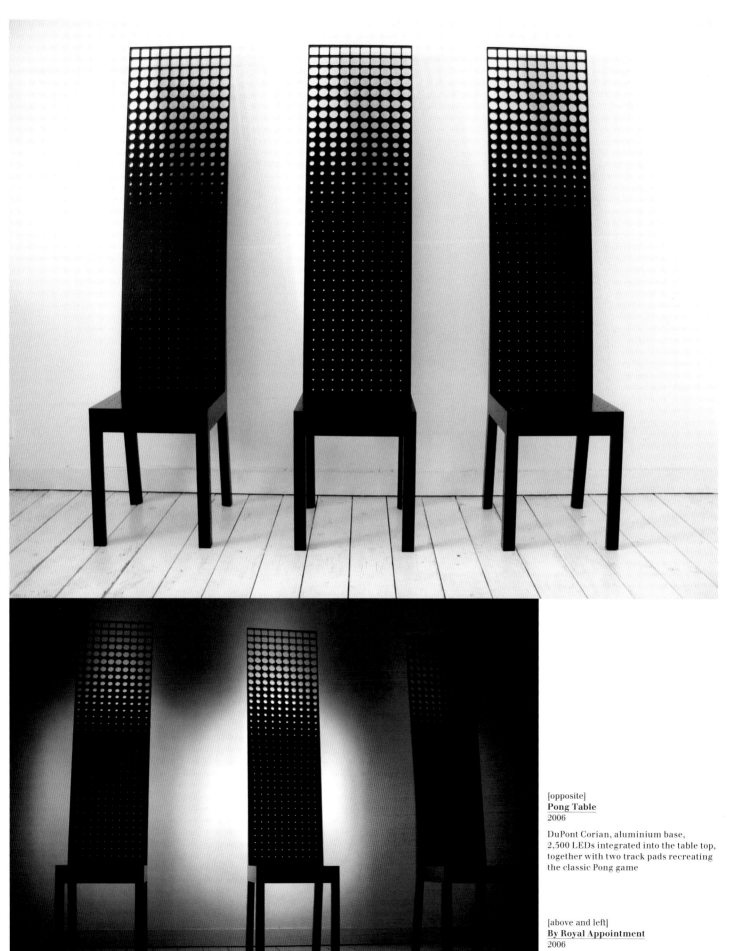

[opposite]
Pong Table
2006

DuPont Corian, aluminium base,
2,500 LEDs integrated into the table top,
together with two track pads recreating
the classic Pong game

[above and left]
By Royal Appointment
2006

Installation at Gallery Libby Sellers
DuPont Corian, LED lighting, London

SONUMBRA
RESPONSIVE ELECTROLUMINESCENT
WOVEN UMBRELLA

BIOWALL
WOVEN STRUCTURE
FOR LIVING PLANTS

LOOP.PH

Set up in 2002 by Rachel Wingfield and Mathias Gmachl, Loop.pH research explores electronically responsive and light-emitting surfaces and structures for the built environment. Their work strongly reflects Wingfield's background as a textile designer, as much as Gmachl's interest in geometry, and explores how digital technology can contribute to textile design and evolve at the cross-roads between technology, craft and natural processes.

This constructed textile approach is at the heart of BioWall, a structure for living plants made of fibre rods shaped in dodecahedra that are joined together. It is also all the more apparent in the innovatively woven canopy of Sonumbra, an outsized parasol crafted as a lacework of hundreds of electroluminescent wires, which is delicately animated in concert with the generated surround sound that completes the installation and in response to visitors' movements. As each strand of the canopy pulses with light, Sonumbra comes to life as a strangely organic artefact. Half marine electric organism, half bolt catcher, it becomes a mesmerizing experience for the viewer wandering unawares or actively gravitating around it.

[above]
BioWall
2006

Springy fibreglass rods

[opposite and left]
Sonumbra
2006

Mowbray Park, Sunderland
Canopy with embedded solar cells

3D DISPLAY CUBE 3D MODULAR SCREEN
JAMES CLAR

Technology has its holy grails, and the 3D display
is surely one of them. Many worldwide corporations
are spending colossal research budgets on creating
the perfect volumetric screen. The techniques
employed are of a breathtaking variety, from simply
stacking LCD screens behind one another to ultra
high-tech, Star Wars-inspired versions, which use
pulsed, infrared lasers to create glowing points of
plasma in the air. Yet few have the appealing
simplicity and stunning straightforwardness of
James Clar's 3D Display Cube, a volumetric display
made of 1,000 single LEDs wired up as a 10 x 10 x 10
matrix. The cubes provide a serial input, allowing
the data to be displayed and manipulated in 3D, and
can be stacked together to create a larger screen.
Inspired by his background in film and animation,
James Clar initially created his 3D cube as an
attempt to display ideas in a way that more closely
resembles how we envision and experience them.

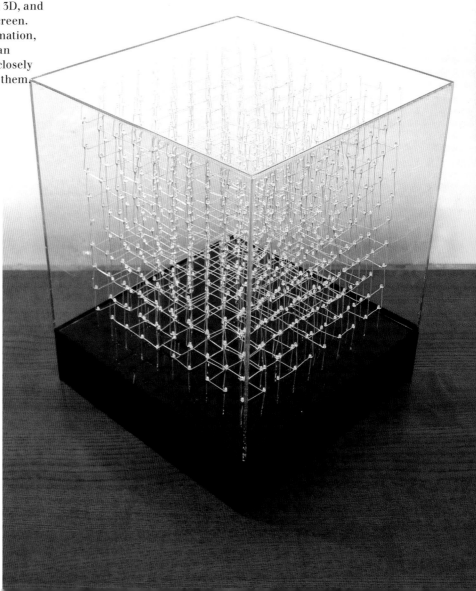

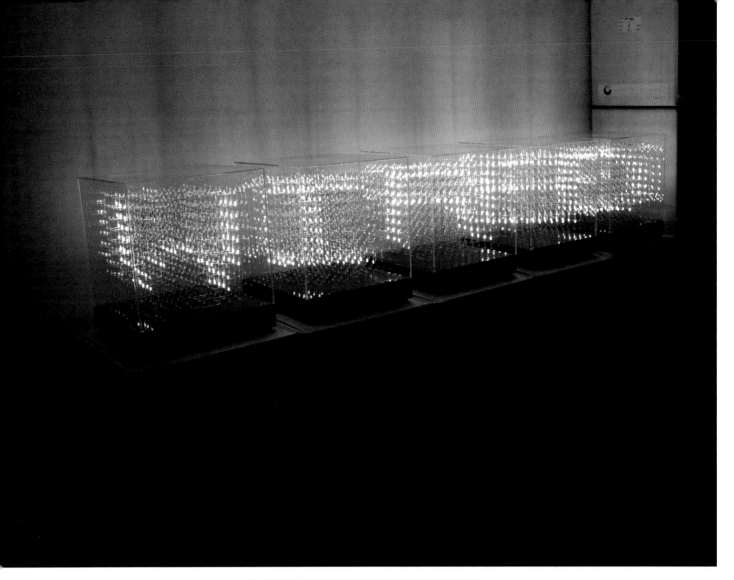

3D Display Cube
2003–6

LEDs, base, microcontrollers
40.6 x 30.5 x 30.5 cm
(16 x 12 x 12 in.)

REED
INTERIOR LIGHTS REACTING
TO OUTSIDE WIND

TREE
INTERACTIVE PROJECTION
IN URBAN SPACES

LIGHTWEEDS
WIND-REACTIVE PROJECTIONS
OF GROWING FLORA

3. RISING

SLOWLY
CHANDELIER SHIMMERING
TO THE OUTSIDE WINDS

SIMON HEIJDENS

Simon Heijdens's work challenges the idea of digital technology as attention-grabbing, eye-catching and instantly gratifying. He eschews the push-button type of interactions and instead seeks a slower, more subtle and meaningful relationship with technology, creating digital objects and installations that are reminiscent of ambient music: calm, almost meditative and slowly evolving in response to their natural environment.

Tree is an interactive digital projection that traces and amplifies the remnants of nature in our planned and controlled urban environment. Connected to a wind sensor, the branches of the projected image blow with the gusts, as if the tree was actually growing there. The projection also becomes a subtle barometer of human activity, as the tree loses one of its leaves each time someone passes by, and the leaves, gently accumulated on the ground, disperse when someone passes through them, creating a poetic reminder of nature and time passing.

Heijdens went a step further with Reed, a group of tall, thin objects that provides both lighting and covering to create muted spots. The reeds translate the natural phenomena occurring outside the building by slowly waving according to the force and direction of the wind throughout the day and through the year. Thus, the installation is calm in summer and intense in autumn. A similar concept is developed in Lightweeds, a series of projections that also responds to the outside winds, but additionally offers a time-based element, as the plants virtually grow.

A similar set-up is explored in 3, Rising Slowly, a chandelier created by Heijdens for Swarovski. Although it has a traditional structure, each of its crystal threads is made of a special memory alloy, which can slightly contract along with the outside wind. This results in a slight shimmer of the crystals as the 'wind' ripples through the chandelier, creating a subtle and slightly surreal feeling of being outside indoors.

Reed
2006

[above]
Lightweeds
New York, 2006

Projectors, computers,
wind/motion sensors

*The projected silhouettes are alive;
they grow depending on actual measured
rainfall and sunshine, move directly on
actual wind and throughout the day turn
along with the sun. The plants are not
pre-drawn or animated, but uniquely
generated by the software and the space
they reside in. A lightweed consists
of several hundred parts that are
independently linked to the sensors
outside, creating a hyper-real motion
that is constantly live-generated.*

[left]
Tree
Porta Venezia, Milan, 2004

Projectors, computers,
wind/motion/sound sensors

[opposite]
3, Rising Slowly
for Swarovski Crystal Palace Collection,
Milan, Italy, 2006

Crystals, reactive thread,
wind sensor

OPEN BURBLE
USMAN HAQUE

GIANT BALLOON CELLULAR
AUTOMATA SCULPTURE

With Burble, experimental architect Usman Haque
offers the public the chance to compete visually
and on an architectural scale with the buildings
that surround them. Not only they will compose
and assemble this giant structure, made of thousands
of illuminated balloons, but they will also be able
to control its flight and perform with it. The giant
organic sculpture sways in the evening air, with
waves of colours rippling on its surface, reaching
for the sky in response to the actions of the crowd
controlling it on the ground. Burble consists of a
large matrix of modular hexagons made of kites'
carbon rods. To each of the 140 hexagons are
attached seven extra-large helium balloons fitted
with a custom-made circuit, which can illuminate
them from the inside. The circuit also contains a
sensor and a small microchip, enabling close-range
communications between the balloons and therefore
the propagation of colour patterns across the
sculpture. To control Burble, the participants hold
and pull on it at ground level, using a series of large
handlebars woven into the hexagonal matrix.
A series of accelerometers is concealed in the bars
to monitor the pulls, subsequently transmitting their
intensity and sequence through an IR signal to the
nearby balloons. This starts an upwards-propagating
colour pulse, as the IR signal is passed on to the
different levels of balloons. There is no central
computer handling the generation of the colour
patterns. Instead, the thousands of individual
circuits behave like a cellular automaton, a semi-
intelligent algorithm the behaviour of which comes
from the discrete computing activites of its elements.
Altering the basic behaviour of each circuit produces
different modes of propagation and interactivity,
resulting in a dynamic, compelling and highly
responsive installation.

Open Burble
Singapore
2006

Constructed from: over 1 km of 0.635 cm
(¼ in.) carbon fibre rods; over 1 km of
Excel D12 high-performance sailing rope;
approx. 1,000 latex balloons (60/90 cm)
(24/35 in.), 1,000 fishing lock-swivel clips,
1,000 Sky Ear boards by Senseinate/Seth
Garlock

*Burble consists of: 30 m (98 ft) of hard
black bamboo and 22 consoles, each
containing an ST Micro triple-axis
accelerometer – the same sensor found
in Nintendo Wii games controllers.*

BATTLES
LIVE-ACTION MUSIC VIDEO FOR
THE WARP FILMS SIGNING

UVA VS CHEMICAL
BROTHERS
GENERATIVE, REAL-TIME GRAPHICS

VOLUME
INTERACTIVE LED INSTALLATION

TRIPTYCH
RESPONSIVE AUDIO-VISUAL
LED INSTALLATION

UNITED VISUAL
ARTISTS

Born out of the VJ scene, United Visual Artists combines art direction, production design and software engineering to deliver real-time responsive visuals and environments, innovatively using computer-controlled lighting technology as sculptural elements. UVA came to prominence through their work for Massive Attack, for whose world tours in 2003 and 2004 they designed the stages. The 100th windows tour (2003) featured a giant LED screen, on which UVA's custom software displayed real-time statistics about the Gulf war, weapons sales or stock market prices, thereby transforming the light show into a moving political statement. Since then, UVA have been creating visuals for numerous bands, as stage lighting, installations or videos. Examples include their stage visuals for the Chemical Brothers in London's Trafalgar Square and their LED installations for a new video for New York progressive rock band Battles. In all their work, UVA have a predilection for large LED screens, which they control through proprietary software, allowing them to display video content across complex tri-dimensional screen arrangements. This software-driven approach can also be read in their visual language, often based on generative algorithms, in an ingenious mixture of art and mathematics.

Recently, UVA brought their unique skills and sensibility to bear on developing more artistic installations, such as Volume, commissioned by Sony Playstation and installed in the sumptuous garden of the Victoria & Albert Museum in London. Volume consists of an array of 46 LED light columns arranged in the centre of the John Madjeski Garden, and which

responds to the visitors' movements with movement of light and sound into the columns. A highly theatrical experience, blissfully executed, it invites you to perform and consider your relationship with your fellow performers. A similar feel was developed in an installation entitled Triptych, created for the Parisian Nuits Blanches art festival.

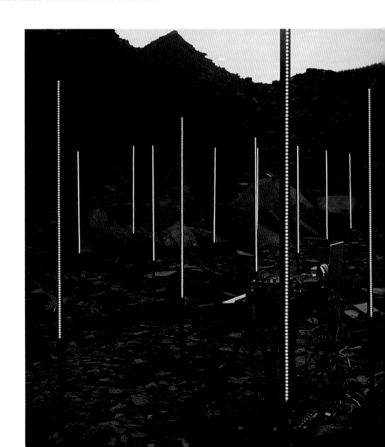

[left]
Battles
2007

Single 'Tonto'
commissioned by Warp Films

[above]
UVA vs Chemical Brothers
Trafalgar Square, 2007

One-off gig as part of the ICA's 60th
anniversary celebrations

[above and left]
Volume
Victoria & Albert Museum
London, 2006–7

Musical collaboration with
One Point Six

[below]
Triptych
2007
Paris, for Nuit Blanche

Premiere at the TodaysArt festival
Sound by Matthias Kispert

BIX
INTERACTIVE CIRCULAR
NEON LIGHTS FAÇADE

SPOTS
INTERACTIVE NEON FAÇADE

REALITIES: UNITED

Realities:united is responsible for the design and
development of the iconic BIX media façade on
the Kunsthaus Graz, the famous organic building
designed in 2003 by Peter Cook and Colin Fournier
of Spacelab. BIX is a matrix of 930 off-the-shelf
fluorescent lamps integrated into the eastern
Plexiglas façade of the Arts Centre. A central
computer can simultaneously adjust the brightness
of each of the lamps, up to 20 times a second,
allowing BIX to display images, animations and
films. Circular fluorescent tubes were chosen over
more high-tech, standard display solutions to allow
the best possible integration, both aesthetic and
physical, of the modular matrix with the building.
They are also more economical, enabling the matrix
to be deployed over the whole riverside façade. The
result is a stunning aesthetic, perfectly in tune with
both the architecture and the cultural mission of the
building. As Tim and Jan Edler put it: 'The BIX
media installation and the Kunsthaus architecture
share a strong symbiotic relationship. The façade
as a display extends the communication range of the
Kunsthaus […] and transmits the internal processes
of the building out into the public.' BIX is also an
experimental laboratory; and whereas most outsized
public screens are mainly the preserve of advertising
with its commercial logic, BIX enables artists to
experiment with a new form of communication
which is deeply in need of finding its own language,
vocabulary and syntax, as it is bound to penetrate
further into our urban surroundings.

A subsequent installation by real:united, Spots,
temporarily invested the inside of the glass façade
of an eleven-storey building on the famous Potzdamer
Platz in Berlin. Here, 1,800 standard fluorescent
fittings are arranged in a computer-controlled
matrix, enabling the display of various media
content. 'The aim is not to conceal the architecture
with a media installation, but rather to implement its
logical continuation by other means,' says Jan Edler.
The installation programmed a series of artistic
interventions by different artists, providing art in
a public space – a unique experimental platform to
explore the cultural relevance and impact of large
screens in city centres. '[Spots] is a place as well
as a building and a medium,' says Tim Edler.

«BUILDINGS COMMUNICATE: THROUGH THEIR ARCHITECTURE AND – AS PART OF THE ARCHITECTONIC CONCEPT – VIA THEIR FAÇADES.»
REALITIES:UNITED

BIX
Communicative Display Skin for the
Kunsthaus Graz
Graz, Austria, 2003

Architects: Spacelab UK
(Peter Cook & Colin Fornier) & ÖBA
Architektur Consult

«THE DYNAMIC SURFACES TURN THE EXTERIOR
SHELL OF A BUILDING INTO A COMMUNICATION
MEDIUM, AN INTERMEDIARY BETWEEN
STRUCTURE AND OUTDOOR SPACE.» REALITIES:UNITED

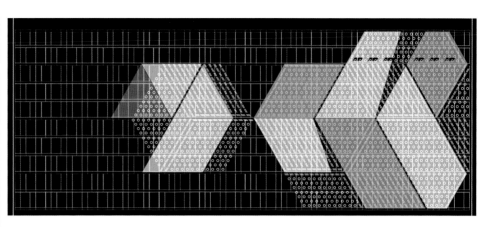

SPOTS Light and Media Installation
Potsdamer Platz, Berlin
2005–7

ALL THE TIME IN
THE WORLD ELECTROLUMINESCENT
ANIMATED WORLD CLOCK
TROIKA

All the Time in the World is a 22-metre (72-foot) electroluminescent installation, which marks the entrance of the British Airways First and Concorde lounges in Heathrow's Terminal 5. It extends the conventional notion of a world clock showing the time in different time zones, by linking real time to places with exciting, exotic or romantic associations. On it you can see the real time in far-distant locations that are home to great natural wonders of the world, such as its highest mountains, as well as such manmade wonders as tall buildings or forgotten ancient cities. It therefore subverts the function of the traditional clock into a poetic, fictional tool, which aims to instil a feeling of travel and set you wondering about the nature of our globalized world.

For All the Time in the World the designers developed a new typology of electroluminescent displays, called Firefly, which relies on a custom-designed segmented typeface, rather like a digital watch, but with many more elements. Not only is it extremely thin, but this display technology can also be curved, boasts extremely low energy consumption (about 700 W for the whole display) and has high aesthetic impact. It has the ability to structure information thanks to the five different fonts that can be shown within the segmented arrangement. The technique is transferable to other emerging technologies such as OLED, PLED or E-paper, and the modular approach also allows the letters to be animated to look as if they were handwritten on to the display.

This installation demonstrates that display technologies need not always be in full colour, full size and full resolution: a simple text display is often all that is needed. However, that is not to say that one solution is supreme – in the future there are likely to be a variety of solutions to meet different challenges.

Another inspiration for the team were early electronic display elements such as nixie tubes, which exhibit a strong physicality and particular light quality, characteristics that give them the edge over more advanced technology. The Firefly elements were used here to bring these sensual qualities into the equation, resulting in a display system at the cross-roads of high- and low-tech – high-tech as it uses emerging printed electronic technologies, but also, being manually silkscreen-printed and restricted to text, letters and cyphers, exuding a distinct, warm, low-tech feel.

All the Time in the World
2008
Electroluminescent wall

3.6 x 22 x 0.001 m
(11 ft 10 in. x 72 ft 2 in. x ¹/₁₆ in.)

Entrance lobby to the British Airways
First and Concorde Galleries Lounges
Heathrow, Terminal 5, London

2/AUGMENTED ART
NARRATIVE TECHNOLOGIES AND IMMERSIVE EXPERIENCES

In Augmented Art, we are looking at a more artistic treatment of technology. This chapter showcases works that explore interactivity and the possibilities opened up by multimedia and electronic technologies to create immersive experiences, integrating complex narrative elements, theatricality and magic in spaces, sculptures or installations. The works exhibit strong human qualities and subjective motivations, as well as demonstrating unique physical qualities, as the artists and designers mix digital thinking with analogue processes and materials, taking media art to the next level and bringing physicality and warmth to a medium that can otherwise often appear cold and immaterial.

MICHAEL CROSS/ 114 JULIUS POPP/ 116 BJÖRN SCHÜLKE/ 118 SACHIKO KODAMA/ 122 PETER VOGEL/ 126 MINIM++/ 130 GREYWORLD/ 132 TATSUO MIYAJIMA/ 134 PAUL DEMARINIS/ 136 TROIKA/ 138

LOOP SYSTEM QUINTET

LIGHT TRACING MACHINE INSPIRED BY HARMONICS AND QUANTUM PHYSICS

PALINDROME

LIGHT TRACING MACHINE DEALING WITH WAVE/PARTICLE DUALITY

BINARY STAR

LIGHT TRACING MACHINE INSPIRED BY BI-SOLAR PLANETARY SYSTEMS

CONRAD SHAWCROSS

The work of Conrad Shawcross is derived from a keen interest in and reflections on science, and in the limits of validity of its main ideas. His structural and often mechanical sculptures reflect an epistemological enquiry, questioning the philosophy behind fundamental science, often taking as starting points controversial theories and scientific paradoxes in the great fields of contemporary research: cosmology, mathematics or quantum theory.

Loop System Quintet is a series of five large, mechanical machines connected by a single drive-shaft, each drawing a different 'knot' of light in space. The resulting patterns, which appear as the machines spin at high speed, are a visual transcription of musical chords and harmonic modes of vibrations described in string theory, a scientific construct that describes the most minute elements of matter as vibrating 'strings'. This theory contradicts the standard model of particle physics, but, if proven, could lead to the theory of everything, the holy grail of science. To this search for the absolute truth, Shawcross adduces his monumental machines, which, behind their perfect and rational construction, have no further rational purpose, thereby forcing us to deduce their raison d'être.

For Binary Star, part of his exhibition entitled 'No Such Thing as One Thing', Shawcross started from the recent discovery of stars locked in orbits around each other, a model opposed to the reality of our own mono-solar system. Binary Star uses a similar aesthetic to the previous piece and stages this binary model as a gigantic machine reproducing the movements of the stars with spinning bulbs. The work, of an electrifying scale and speed, reveals the symmetries of this unfamiliar phenomenon.

Shawcross's obsessive questioning of the veracity of science continues with Palindrome, a machine tracing opposing spirals in space, which could be read as an attempt at visualizing the classic duality of wave/particle, a theory that describes quantum elements and light either as grains of matter or as waves of energy. It could also be plausibly interpreted as an illustration of the infamous EPR paradox, a complex paradox in quantum physics that has perplexed scientists for many years.

[opposite]
Loop System Quintet
2005

Waxed machined oak, five light bulbs, electric motor and gearbox, drive shafts, cogs, universal joints, flange units, screws, bolts, nuts, washers
3 x 17 x 17 m
(9 ft 10 in. x 55 ft 9 in. x 55 ft 9 in.)

[above]
Studio

[left and overleaf]
Binary Star
2006

Mixed media
Diameter 9 m (29 ft 6 in.)

[above]
Palindrome
2007

Aluminium, steel,
mechanical parts, lights

[left]
Loop System Quintet
2005

Waxed machined oak, 5 x light bulbs,
electric motor and gearbox, drive shafts,
cogs, universal joints, flange units, screws,
bolts, nuts, washers
3 x 17 x 17 m
(9 ft 10 in. x 55 ft 9 in. x 55 ft 9 in.)

MECHANICAL MIRRORS
INTERACTIVE ELECTRONIC MIRRORS WITH ANALOGUE PIXELS
DANIEL ROZIN

Among the most beautiful examples of tangible technology, Rozin's mechanical mirror series presents us with striking examples of a digital technology that has the warmth of analogue media. Each mirror in the series is composed of hundreds of physical fragments, rather like analogue 'pixels', which can move individually to reconstitute the images that appear before them. A video camera sited in the middle of each mirror is linked to a computer, which controls the individual pixels.

For Wooden Mirror, the 'pixels' are composed of little wooden blades that can rotate horizontally thanks to a dedicated servo motor. Depending on their inclinations, the wooden blades will catch more or less of the light cast by a spot positioned on top of the mirror and shining down on them. Different contrasts can be obtained in this way and, by controlling the inclination of all 900 blades, a grey-scale mirror image is created.

Standing in front of such a mirror and seeing one's reflection in a wooden surface is a compelling and mesmerizing experience, heightened by the rustling noise made by the moving blades.

A similar technique is explored in Rozin's later Peg Mirror. Here, 650 circular wooden cylindrical pieces are cut on an angle and can rotate individually, catching different amounts of light to create the required grey scale. By controlling the precise rotation of each peg, the master software recreates the image.

Circles Mirror introduces another principle to the mirror series by using hundreds of circular discs printed with elaborate patterns – specifically developed and printed by Rozin – whose darkness evolves angularly. The grey shades are obtained by rotation, the disc thereby exhibiting a lighter or darker portion of its prints as required.

Weave Mirror, another recent piece, continues Rozin's printmaking efforts, this time using laminated C-shaped prints along the surface of the picture plane. The C-shapes are arranged in a way that texturally mimics a homespun basket, hence the name of the mirror. Informed by traditions of both textile design and new media, the mirror paints a picture of the viewer using a gradual rotation in grey-scale value on each C-ring.

[opposite]
Circles Mirror
2005

Laminated circles, motors, computer,
video camera, custom software
152 x 152 x 15 cm (60 x 60 x 6 in.)
Edition of 6

[below]
Circles Mirror
2005

Detail view

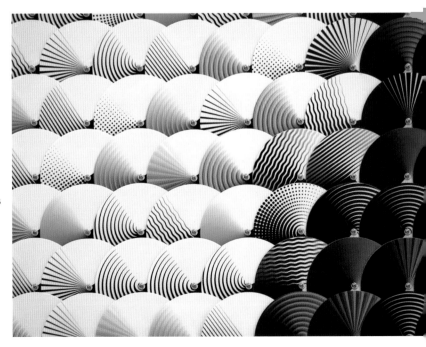

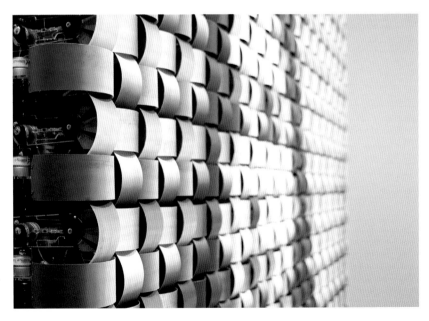

[above]
Weave Mirror
2007

768 laminated C-ring prints, motors,
circuits, custom software, microcontroller
148 x 193 x 20 cm (58 x 76 x 8 in.)
Edition of 6

[left]
Weave Mirror
2007

Detail view

[above]
Wooden Mirror
1999

Wood, computer, video, various circuitry,
custom software
155 x 178 x 20 cm (61 x 70 x 8 in.)
framed
Edition of 6

[left]
Peg Mirror
2007

650 cylindrical wood pieces, motors,
circuits, custom software, microcontroller
Diameter 104 cm (41 in.),
depth 17.8 cm (7 in.)
Edition of 10

LISTENING
POST
ELECTRONIC INSTALLATION
WHICH LISTENS TO THE INTERNET

MARK HANSEN &
BEN RUBIN

Born out of the unusual collaboration between
an artist, Ben Rubin, and a statistics expert, Mark
Hansen, the Listening Post is a sublime, highly
theatrical art installation conceived as a visual
and sonic response to the content, magnitude and
immediacy of virtual communication. It works by
culling text fragments in real time from thousands
of unrestricted internet chat rooms, bulletin
boards and other public forums. The texts are then
read (or sung) by several voice synthesizers and
simultaneously displayed across a suspended grid
of more than 200 small vacuum fluorescent
electronic screens.

Listening Post cycles through a series of six
movements, each with a different arrangement
of visual, aural and musical elements, and its
own data processing logic. In one movement, for
instance, it will track all the messages that are
written at that minute starting with 'I am...'.
It feels like hearing the whole of humanity in
one go, a giant cut-up poem made of 100,000
different versions of the same, exposing the fears
and uncertainties of real people, and all typed
only seconds before.

The set-up and theatrical arrangement of the
installation, exquisitely executed, contribute greatly
to the impact of what could be called a performance
piece, always unique, played by plentiful anonymous
actors. The voices are rich in tone and it is hard to
believe that they emanate from the complex network
of four computers that run the Listening Post.
Extreme attention to detail has been paid to every
element of the movements and their music, as well
as the physical design of the piece itself. Each screen
has even been fitted with a kind of ticker, which
enables the displays to become part of the soundtrack,
enhancing the musical component with physical
percussive ticking that is reminiscent of older display
technology and can be used to add a dramatic,
cinematic feeling by moving the sound across the
200 screens of the installation. The Listening Post
is a truly amazing piece, which sets the benchmark
for internet-based art.

[below and opposite]
Listening Post
2001–3

«FROM ITS CONCEPTION, LISTENING POST HAS BEEN
A PRODUCT OF OUR COMBINED TALENTS. THE SPACE
IS AS MUCH ABOUT AN ARTISTIC EXPRESSION AS IT IS
DATA ANALYSIS.» MARK HANSEN

Listening Post
2001–3

«I USED TO WONDER
WHETHER IT MIGHT BE
POSSIBLE TO HEAR THE
SOUNDS OF ANCIENT
POTTERS CHATTING BY
'PLAYING' THE GROOVES
FORMED ON POTS
THROWN A THOUSAND
YEARS AGO. FOR YEARS,
I HAVE THOUGHT ABOUT
WAYS TO HEAR INAUDIBLE
PHENOMENA, WAYS TO
MAP THE OBSERVABLE
WORLD INTO THE SOUND
DOMAIN.» BEN RUBIN

STANDARDS AND DOUBLE STANDARDS
INTERACTIVE INSTALLATION
WITH BELTS THAT TURN
TOWARDS YOU

SYNAPTIC CAGUAMAS
BEER BOTTLES THAT
SPIN ACCORDING TO
NEURAL NETWORK LOGIC

WAVEFUNCTION
RESPONSIVE
WAVES
OF CHAIRS

RAFAEL LOZANO-HEMMER

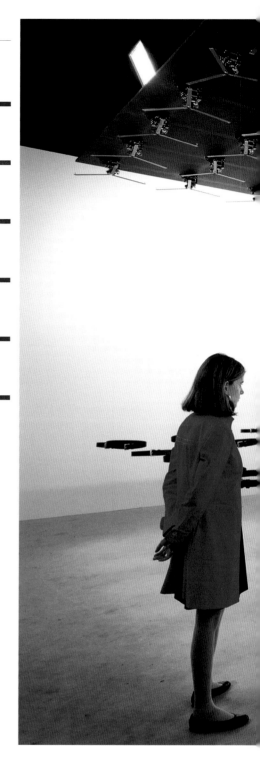

Mexican-born Lozano-Hemmer is an electronic artist who develops interactive installations at the intersection between architecture and performance art. His main interest is in creating platforms for public participation by perverting advanced technologies such as robotics, computerized surveillance or telematic networks, in a poetic and critical way. Between analogue and digital, his hardware-heavy installations usually consist of simple, individually controlled elements repeated in large arrays and coupled with artificially intelligent software to create complex emerging behaviours that mimic organic systems, both within the pieces themselves and in the reactions of the audience.

Synaptic Caguamas is an array of 30 Caguama-style beer bottles, disposed on a large Mexican cantina table. Thanks to the 30 networked stepper motors concealed underneath the table top, the bottles can spin on themselves, displaying patterns generated by a cellular automata algorithm. This is a kind of software that simulates the behaviours of neuronal connections in the brain and approaches coding as the repetition and interaction of small pieces of interrelated code, each linked to a particular bottle, rather than a fixed, global algorithm controlling all the bottles together. Every few minutes the bottles are reset and seeded with new initial conditions for the algorithm so that new, ever-changing movement patterns can emerge. The bottles thus create a magical and fascinating

Standards and Double Standards
2004
Subsculpture 3

Suspended belts, motors, computer,
custom software, screen
Dimensions variable
Edition of 3

spectacle, materializing, as Hemmer intended, the mathematics of recollection and thought.

Standards and Double Standards relies on similar principles and integrates another component in the interaction with the viewer. Here, 50 fastened belts are suspended at waist height from the ceiling and controlled by stepper motors. Informed by a computerized tracking system, the belts rotate automatically to follow the public, turning their buckles slowly to face passers-by. When several people are in the room, their presence affects the entire group of belts, creating chaotic patterns of interference. Non-linear behaviours emerge, displaying turbulence, eddies and relatively quiet regions, similar to those observed in a weather chart. One of the aims of this piece is to visualize complex dynamics, turning a condition of pure surveillance into an unpredictable connective system. An 'absent crowd' interacts with the viewer's own presence and creates a complex feeling between discomfort and enjoyment.

His latest installation to date, premiered at the 52nd Biennale in Venice in 2007, mixes the two approaches. Entitled Wavefunction, the kinetic sculpture comprises classic Eames chairs placed in a 9 x 4 array, facing the entrance to the exhibition space. When someone approaches the work, a computerized surveillance system detects their presence and the closest chairs automatically begin to lift off the ground, creating the crest of a wave that then spreads over the whole array. A system of electro-mechanical pistons softly raises each chair up to forty centimetres from the ground. The pistons are controlled by a computer that runs a mathematical model based on fluid dynamics, thus making the waves interfere with each other, generating turbulence or becoming calm, just like real water.

[above]
Synaptic Caguamas
2004
Subsculpture 4

Glass bottles, wood table, motors, computer, custom software
Dimensions variable
Edition of 3

[opposite]
Wavefunction
2007
Mexican Pavilion, 52nd Venice Biennale

Electromechanical pistons, computers, chairs, surveillance cameras and circuits
Dimensions variable
Edition of 3

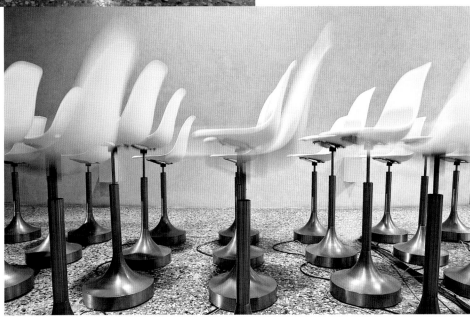

DIVIDE   A SEA OF LEDS

HOME MOVIE

300-1   LOW-RES FILM PROJECTED
BY INVERTED LEDS

HOME MOVIE

608-1   LOW-RES FILM PROJECTED
BY INVERTED LEDS
– LARGE FORMAT

JIM CAMPBELL

Jim Campbell's work explores the distinction between analogue and digital as a metaphor for human ability for poetic understanding, as opposed to the cold, abstract mathematics of data. Often employing LEDs as base material, his pixelated representations are of such a low resolution as to place them at the threshold of recognition. Typically, the viewer will not instantly recognize what is displayed, and it is only after a few seconds of observation that his brain will reconstitute the images into a complete, meaningful idea. This experience is enabled by unique, artful analogue treatments of the digitally driven LED panels, which have become the signature of the artist.

For Divide, Campbell angles a diffusing sheet of acrylic vertically in front of a low-resolution LED panel that displays a short film of ocean waves crashing on a shore, from the top to the bottom of the image. The diffuser will keep the top of the image as the discrete dots formed by the LEDs, while gradually blurring them as the waves reach the bottom of the image, morphing the image into a continuous one. This ingenious and simple treatment metaphorically represents the passage from a digital image, which is hard to make sense of, to an analogue one, which strangely gives us the clues to understand what we are looking at. The experience, which partly relies on our voyeuristic tendencies, feels highly poetic and strangely personal, as if we were the only one to have decoded the images.

With his Home Movie series, Jim Campbell goes a step further in abstracting the data. Here, strung columns of high-powered LEDs are mounted on wires and placed facing the wall, about 8 centimetres away from it. This results in an extremely blurred and low-resolution image, which is further obstructed from view by the strings and LED boards that are placed

between the viewer and the image. After a few seconds of observation, however, the viewer will suddenly make sense of the images displayed. The work displays found footage of home movies low enough in resolution to convey a universal meaning.

[opposite]
Divide
2005

70 x 60 cm (27 x 24 in.) low-resolution LED panel, sheet of diffusing Plexiglas

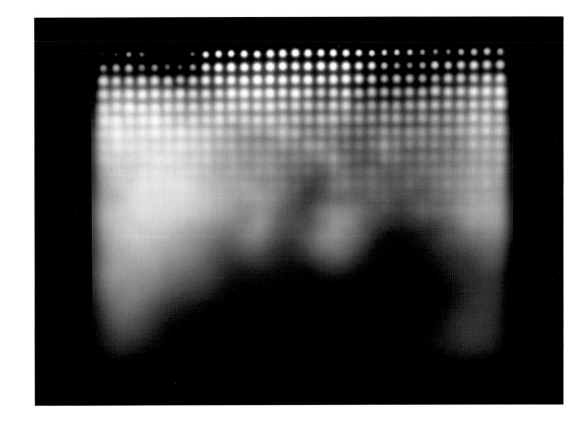

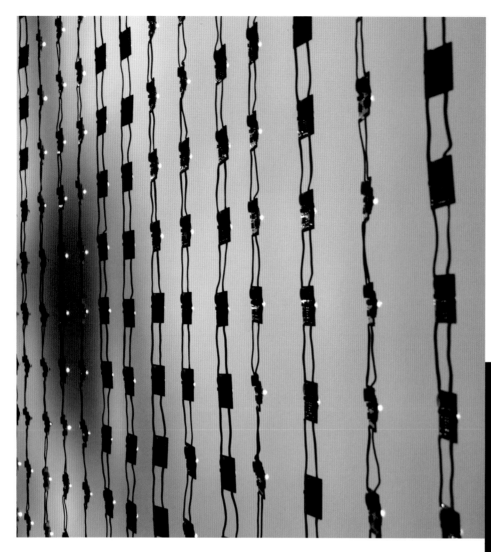

[left, bottom left]
Home Movie 300-1
2006

Strung columns of high-powered LEDs,
7 cm (3 in.) away from the wall

[below and opposite]
Home Movie 608-1
2006

Strung columns of high-powered LEDs,
15 cm (6 in.) away from the wall
3.7 x 4.9 m (12 ft 1 in. x 16 ft 1 in.)

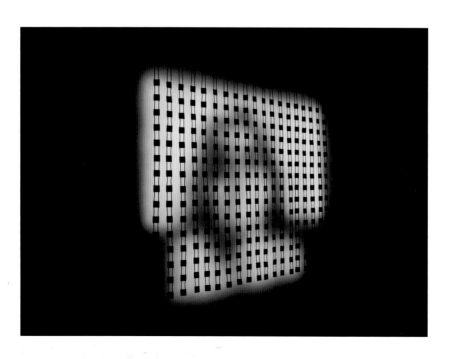

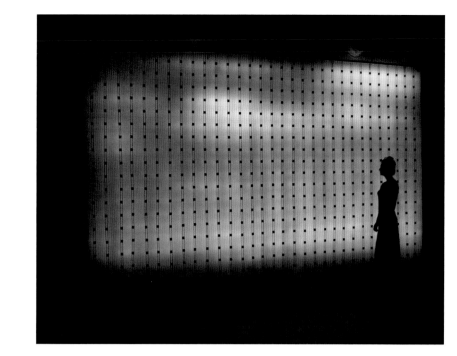

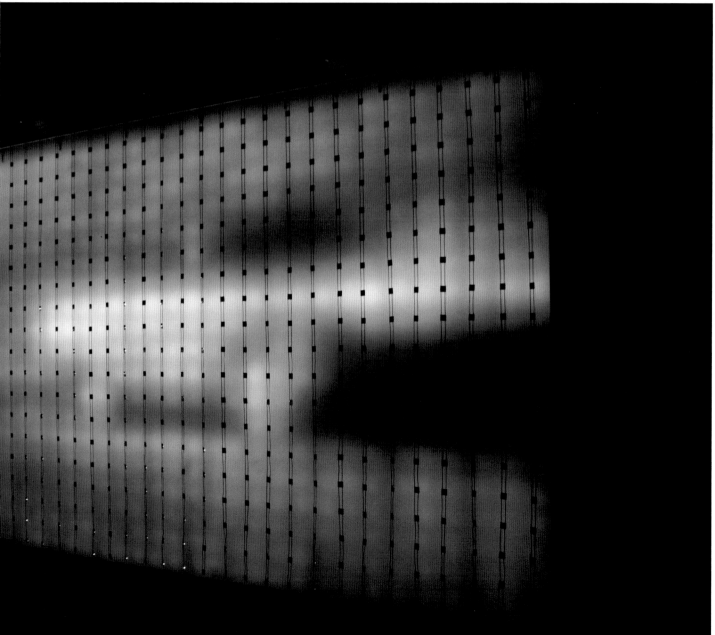

MOVING NEON CUBE
PHYSICAL NEON
ANIMATION SCULPTURE

WALKING CUBE
REACTIVE
MOVING CUBE

CHANGING NEON SCULPTURE
DECEIVINGLY EVOLVING
NEON SCULPTURE

JEPPE HEIN

Like many artists working with technology, Berlin-based Jeppe Hein is interested by its capacity to challenge our expectations of what an artwork can be. But Hein's technologically enhanced pieces present us with a novel and refined conception of interactivity, where the link between the viewer's behaviour and the response from the artwork is neither obvious nor immediate, leaving the viewer in the position of spectator/actor despite himself, and drawing him in unawares, in a cunning, passive-aggressive way.

Hein's pieces also often play with the heritage of minimalism, humorously mocking the modern notion that the artwork exists without the viewer, in favour of a more theatrical approach. His formal vocabulary often uses the archetypical cube, the most abstract and stable form of all, which starts to perform in various and surprising ways. In Moving Neon Cube, the minimalist shape is freed of its staticity. The sculpture consists of twelve neon cubes chained together in the shape of a large square on the ground, and angled to create the impression of a rolling cube. The different cubes are then lit in sequence to give the impression of a single cube rolling in a continuous loop, in a kind of chronosculpture reminiscent of Etienne-Jules Marey's chronophotography.

Walking Cube is another example: when activated by the visitor's presence, the cube flips by itself from one side to the other and repeats the action one more time before stopping. Here, because the work can be activated at intervals only, the visitor is left perplexed, lacking any explanation for this strange phenomenon. Changing Neon Sculpture, a volumetric matrix of 3 x 3 x 3 neon cubes, plays on similar principles. The illumination of the cubes changes every two seconds, displaying a sequence of different consistent forms,

such as pyramids, stairs, etc., thus creating a new light sculpture each time. Here, the visitor's presence is tracked and the cube freezes its light movement as soon as a visitor approaches, to resume only when she has left.

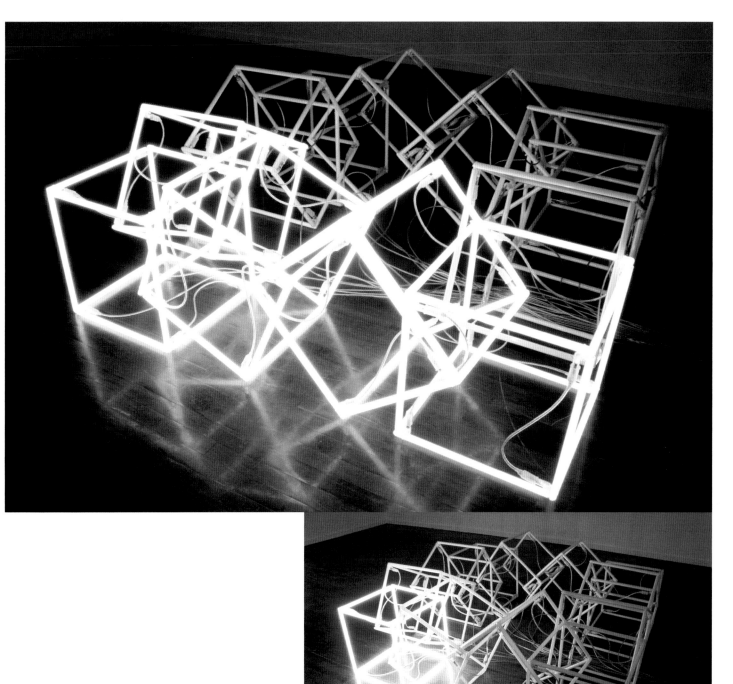

[above]
Moving Neon Cube
2004

Neon tubes, transformer
70 x 250 x 250 cm (27 x 98 x 98 in.)

[opposite]
Walking Cube
2004

Aluminium, electrical motor, battery,
sensor, technical apparatus
50 x 50 x 50 cm (20 x 20 x 20 in.)

Changing Neon Sculpture
2006

Neon tubes, transformer, sensor,
control technics
150 x 150 x 150 cm (59 x 59 x 59 in.)

ROBOTIC
CHAIR
SELF-DESTRUCTING AND
EVER RE-ASSEMBLING CHAIR

MAX DEAN,
RAFFAELLO
D'ANDREA,
MATT DONOVAN

At first sight, the Robotic Chair looks ordinary
enough. But suddenly, its legs start to wobble and
the chair collapses on the floor with shuddering
force. Then, with persistence and determination,
the robot concealed in the chair's seat will proceed
to seek out the different parts, to rebuild the chair
and come back to its upright position, using its legs
as a lift, before collapsing again, endlessly. Watching
this Sisyphean robot rebuilding itself again and again
elicits in the viewer a complex feeling of empathy,
compassion and hope. The chair was chosen for its
status as a trustworthy partner in the history of civil
society. It stands as a metaphor for the individual and
a society over the course of a lifetime – falling apart
in pieces, gathering oneself together and rising up
again and again – reminding us that on a grand
scale, there is magic and hope.

Originally imagined by artist Max Dean in 1984,
it took over twenty years to design and build the
current version of this near-impossible object,
with the collaboration of automation engineer
Pr. Raffaello d'Andrea and Matt Donovan, an artist
with an innate sense for engineering. The robot
housed in the chair's seat is controlled by a computer
vision system located overhead.

Robotic Chair
1984–2006

ONDULATION
THOMAS MCINTOSH

The visualization of sound has been the subject of numerous works of design and art, but Ondulation – originally created by Canadian artist Thomas McIntosh, composer Emmanuel Madan and scenic artist Mikko Hynninen – ranks certainly among the most beautiful and elaborate pieces on the theme.

Ondulation is a composition for water, sound and light. In a room plunged into semi-darkness, the water in a large basin ripples as waves radiate across its surface, ad infinitum, with perfect mathematical purity. Intuitively, you know that the sounds around you are closely related to the ripples, a fact reinforced by the water's movements reflected on the surrounding walls by a sophisticated play of light. Two powerful speakers, concealed beneath the elastic lining of the pool, allow for the sonic vibrations to be transmitted into the fluid, thus creating the physical waves of water travelling across the pool. The height and speed of the waves are directly linked to the volume and frequency of the sound in the exciters. The sound output controls the choreography of the waves. Because the pool has no apparent borders for the water – as the fluid can simply flow over the edges – the pool behaves like an infinite plane and no reflected waves can come to disturb the composition. It is a piece of extreme beauty, the subliminal purity of which was achieved only thanks to a profound understanding of the medium and a mastery of the technology following a long series of experiments.

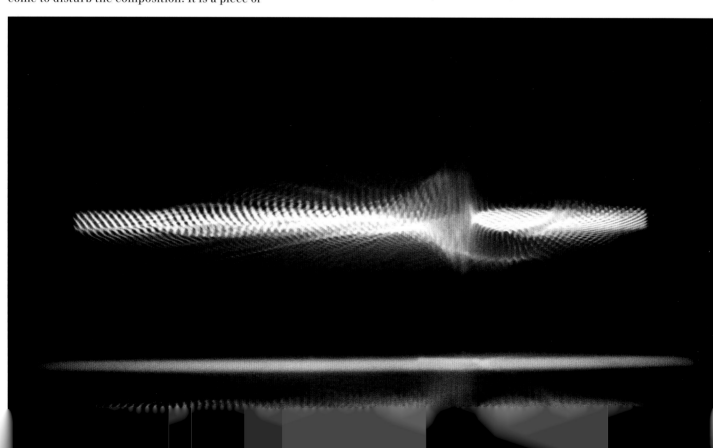

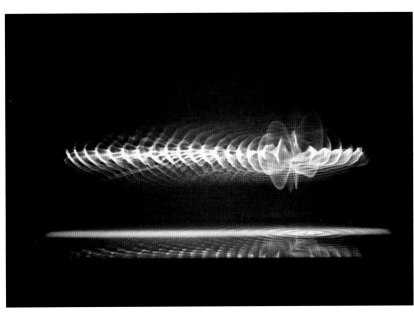

Ondulation
2002

3 x 4 m (9 ft 10 in. x 13 ft 1 in.)

Installation version

Ondulation
Montreal Museum
of Contemporary Art,
Montreal, 2005

SHOWTIME

LED LAP DANCER
ANIMATION

SARA DANCING
(SPARKLY TOP)

SARA ON A
LED COLUMN

BRUCE & SUZANNE
WALKING

LED FIGURES WALKING
ON A RIVER

JULIAN OPIE

The world of Julian Opie, one of the leading figures of British contemporary art, is populated by an intricate community of cartoon characters, which he most famously depicts in portraits, using his signature pop and minimal style characterized by clear lines and uniform fields of colour. From Kiera the artist to Hughes the investor, Keith the mechanic to Kate the model, all of Opie's characters are based on real people but simplified to their essence, until the character sits on the border between the particular and the universal, presenting the complexity of the human form reduced to its basics. To achieve this, Opie draws over photographs or short films of his models using computer software, reducing the details in the original material until he obtains his diagrammatic figures.

Following the same principle, Opie also creates animations of his characters, which have a minimum of detail but reveal the identity and presence of the model by way of stance, clothes and movements. Those minimal animations are thought as short loops that play continuously and Opie displays them on a variety of supports, from plasma screens to life-size to double-sided monochromatic LED displays.

With his animation of Bruce the dancer and Suzanne the fashion designer walking on the Vltava, Opie displays his innate ability to create extraordinary fluidity of movement. The choice of the display method is also an integral part of the piece, as the crudeness of the monochromatic LED – a technology usually reserved for signage – echoes the minimal aesthetic of the characters, while further contrasting with the poetry of the surroundings and the elegance of the movements. Opie's entrancing minimalist animated sculptures are an inspiration in a world obsessed with large, full-colour, full-resolution, outdoor display technology.

[opposite]
SHOWTIME
2006

Installation view from
Gallery Bob Van Orsouw, 2006

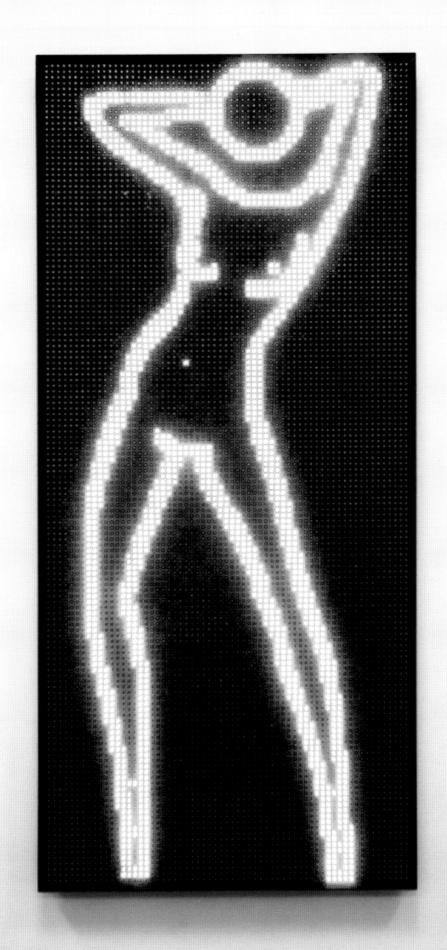

«OPIE REALLY DOES SEEM TO US THE PAINTER
OF OUR MODERN LIFE, A LIFE IN WHICH THE
REAL AND THE VIRTUAL, THE ARTIFICIAL AND
THE AUTHENTIC, FEELINGS AND LOGOS ARE
ALL MIXED.» JUAN MANUEL BONET

[above]
Sara Dancing (Sparkly Top)
2004

Installation view from
Indianapolis, 2006

[above]
Bruce & Suzanne Walking

Installation view from River Vltava,
Prague, 2007

MACHINE
#1.4
SPACE-SHIFTING
KINETIC SCULPTURE
JAMES CARRIGAN

James Carrigan's interdisciplinary practice draws on both fine art and radical design to create works in which space and its mediation lie at the core. With his Machine series, he explores the relationship with both the work and its viewing context, the machines becoming the central components of architectural interventions within the gallery, where parallel states of existence between the space and the viewer are explored.

Machine #1.4 is a sculpture, a kinetic installation and a form of architecture, created to transform the space of the room, while subjecting its viewer to a multisensory, emotional experience. A kind of giant automated puppeteer machine, the installation consists of 30 triangulated aluminium arms radiating from a central hub and mounted to the ceiling of the gallery. Each arm supports one to three pulley systems, each controlling, via 160 colour-coded steel cables, one of 40 suspended, triangular, ceramic foam panels. At rest, the ceramic foam panels form a delicate, translucent, floating geodesic dome that fills the space of the gallery. The dome evokes associations of a shelter, an intimate and protective environment in which to find oneself and create new thoughts.

The machine rests in this configuration for one hour, after which the ceramic panels slowly move outwards while levelling and ascend towards the ceiling, a process lasting about seven minutes. The movement is almost imperceptible but for the panels gently scraping against each other and generating a sharp but delicate echoing sound that fills the gallery. During the transformation, one can witness the purity of the mathematical construction exploding in chaotic shards of fragmented ceramic panes, altering drastically our perception of the room and its space, while leaving us with an altogether different object to contemplate. The panels rest in their chaotic position overhead for one hour before the machine reverses and returns the panels to their geodesic position. In total autonomy, the machine repeats this process for the duration of the whole exhibition, endlessly exploding and imploding.

Machine #1.4
2005

BRIDGE

ONEIRIC 'WALK ON
THE WATER' BRIDGE

MICHAEL CROSS

As you enter a disused concrete church, your eyes
are greeted by a giant pool of deep, dark water
covering most of the floor space. One clue only –
a small staircase that seems to finish in the water
itself. Reaching the top of the stairs unleashes the
magic, as a small wooden step suddenly rises from
the depth, inviting you to continue your walk on the
water itself. As you do, another step emerges. There
is no point in turning back from your intriguing
journey: as the steps emerge in front of you, they also
disappear behind. The displacement of your body
weight makes the steps rise and fall...until you
reach the middle of the pool, 30 steps and 12 metres
(39 feet 4 inches) off the shore.

With Bridge, artist and experimental designer
Michael Cross invites you to a dreamlike experience,
slightly frightening, intensely magical and physically
involving: it evokes complex feelings, both as an idea
and as an adventure. It involves trust in your balance
and in the mechanism itself. Originally created in
the Grade II church of Dilston Grove, London, the
cavenous yet peaceful context lends great reverence
to the idea of walking on water.

Like most of Cross's work, Bridge is at once
powerfully engaging and disturbing. It is the first
piece in a new series of installations of seemingly
absurd and dreamlike scenarios, which Cross
intends as genuine propositions for the real world.
With his highly inspirational works, Cross uses
otherwise purely functional objects to appeal to
our fantasies and thus confront us with our reality.

Bridge
Dilston Grove, 2006

Steel, mechanical components, water

BIT.FLOW
FLOWING LIQUID DISPLAY

BIT.FALL
CONTROLLED RAIN DISPLAY

JULIUS POPP

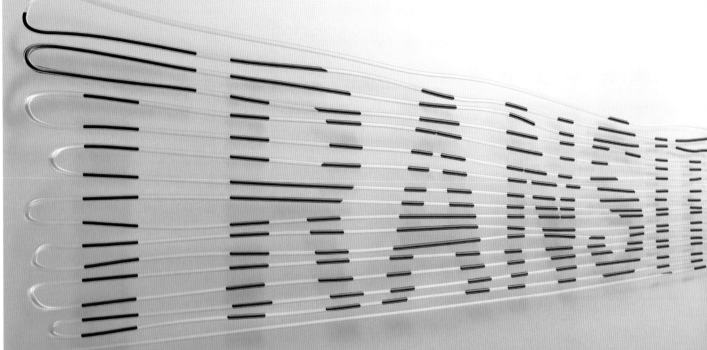

Artist Julius Popp works at the cross-roads between art and science. With Bit.fall, Popp creates an automated display made of rain, applying the logical rules of the machines to a natural phenomenon in order to create a water curtain that can display text and images: 320 nozzles, controlled via computer software by electromagnetic valves, emit individual drops of water. Bit.fall manages precisely to control the drops as they fall to the ground, creating 8-metre (26-foot 3-inch) wide bitmap patterns, in a sort of giant water printer. As the images dissolve, the water drops are collected in a container on the ground, underneath the nozzles, and pumped back into the system. In its current set-up, Bit.fall displays buzzwords selected by a statistics-based computer program from various internet news websites.

Aside from its incredible technical prowess, Bit.fall can be read as a critical commentary on our society's permanent quest to achieve an objectifiable representation of reality by means of technological advances. It is a metaphor for the incessant and transient flow of information that assails us, of which we constantly try to make sense and from which we draw our perpetually changing realities.

In a second installation, Bit.flow, Popp furthers this continuous interplay between order and chaos. Here at a prototype stage, immiscible liquids are pumped through a 45-metre (147-foot 8-inch) long tube laid out on a wall. A transparent liquid serves as an invisible carrier while a tinted one forms drops or lines, as an equivalent of one or several pixels. By means of a motion-tracking device, a computer program imposes order on the chaos, pumping the fluids into the tube in controlled measures to form linear patterns that create a meaningful image only at one point in time, when the entire pattern is contained in the tube. As the flow is constant, each image immediately disintegrates into chaos.

[opposite]
Bit.flow
2004–5
Prototype

Pumps, electronic components,
45 m (147 ft 8 in.) tygon tubes, silicon ak100,
coloured water

[above and left]
Bit.fall
2001–6

Water, pump, electronic valves,
electronic components

PLANET SPACE
ROVER
REACTIVE ROBOTIC
SCULPTURE

ORGAMAT
SOUND ROBOTIC
SCULPTURE

DRONE # 6
SURVEILLANCE ROBOTIC
SCULPTURE

SOLAR KINETIC
OBJECT # 28
SOLAR-POWERED
KINETIC ROBOT

BJÖRN SCHÜLKE

Björn Schülke creates interactive sculptures in which media art mixes with kinetic in a unique, tri-dimensional language. Born out of a world of spaceships, 1960s science fiction and unusual scientific instruments, his sculptures appear both fragile and elegant, and manage, beyond their inherent playfulness, to question the way we interact with modern technologies – more specifically with robotics, interactive technologies and surveillance.

With his Drone series, Schülke considers the apprehension and paranoia that beset us in our dealings with surveillance devices. His Drone 6 hangs from the ceiling, presenting itself as a playful, futuristic and beautifully executed robot. Integrated in the device is a LCD monitor displaying what the drone sees, and a little propeller mounted on an extended arm, which allows the drone to rotate as it scans the room. The drone also incorporates two cameras and a heat sensor to enable it to track a human presence. The viewer's discomfiture under this constant observation deepens the meaning of the piece. Another example of what Schülke calls an 'autonomous observation device' is his Planet Space Rover, a large, kinetic robot fitted with similar equipment, which responds by movements to a human presence. The robot also integrates a long-wave scanner to extend its range of observation.

Orgamat, an audio–video sculpture, transforms insipid daily TV shows into the warm and melodious sounds of five organ pipes. There, five sensors stuck on to an integrated TV screen detect the light intensity in the pictures, permitting control of the pipes. But beyond the darker readings of Schülke's

work remains a distinct feeling that the artist loves the technology, its forms and possibilities, an attitude that finds expression in works such as his solar kinetic objects, smaller kinetic devices that are self-powered by means of embedded solar cells.

Planet Space Rover
2004

Fibreglass, wood, metal, motors, sensors,
cameras and solar cells
292 x 150 x 150 cm (115 x 59 x 59 in.)

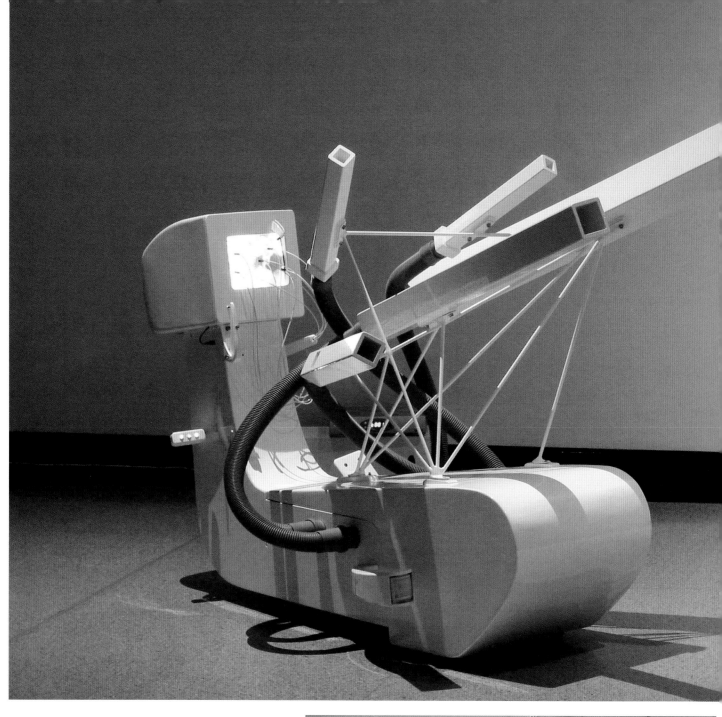

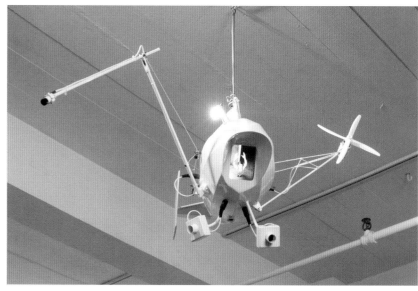

[opposite top]
Orgamat
2003

Wood, metal, electronics, television,
fan, paint
119 x 170 x 89 cm (47 x 67 x 35 in.)

[opposite bottom]
Drone #6
2006

Fibreglass, plywood, aluminium, colour
monitor, two cameras, motors, infrared
sensor, halogen light
64 x 71 x 71 cm (25 x 28 x 28 in.)

[above]
Solar Kinetic Object #28
2006

Solar cells, motor, brass wire, circuits,
automotive paint
15 x 20 x 14 cm (6 x 8 x 5 in.)

EQUILIBRIUM POINT
SHAPE-SHIFTING MAGNETIC
FLUID SCULPTURE

PULSATE
RESPONSIVE INSTALLATION

PROTRUDE, FLOW
MOVING
MAGNETIC
FLUID

SACHIKO KODAMA

With her series of work using magnetic fluid, Japanese artist Sachiko Kodama taps into another technological dream: a material whose shape can be remotely and dynamically controlled. The dense, enigmatic black fluid that Kodama repeatedly uses is a ferro-fluid, made by dissolving microscopic iron powder in oil. It remains strongly magnetic in its fluid state and can therefore be shaped by the powerful magnetic fields generated by computer-controlled electromagnets.

In her first installation, Protrude, Flow, created together with Minako Takeno, the black fluid allows the viewer to witness the sheer wonder and complexity of the magnetic force fields, produced by six independent electromagnets. The sound level in the room directly controls the relative force of each magnet, imposing different configurations on the magnetic field, thus animating the fluid in a series of awe-inspiring shapes. A camera also captures the moving magnetic fluid and projects it, enlarged, on to a screen in the gallery. Because of the liquid nature of the sculpted medium, Protrude, Flow serves as a kind of window on another world, enabling us to see a natural phenomenon normally hidden from our perception.

Kodama refined this novel aesthetic principle in a later piece, Equilibrium Point. Here, the machine itself is refined as an integral part of the sculpture, and the video projection is abandoned. The sound reactiveness of the early piece is still present, but in a slower, less chaotic form, letting the magnetic fluid shape reach a state of equilibrium where the gravity of the fluid, the magnetic force and the environmental sounds equalize.

In Pulsate, she places the fluid in a more theatrical context, on a large white dish in the centre of a dinner table, among ordinary tableware objects. The floor is covered with white sand, and the room filled with intense fluorescent white light. While people gather around the installation, the black fluid slowly

pulsates in sync with the environmental noise, until it eventually overflows and splashes out of the dish if the sound becomes too loud. The animated fluid becomes a kind of ghostly protagonist, a manifestation of another world, a feeling echoed by the emptiness of the chairs and clinical whiteness of the setting.

[below]
Pulsate
2002
In collaboration with Minako Takeno

[opposite]
Equilibrium Point
2003
In collaboration with Minako Takeno

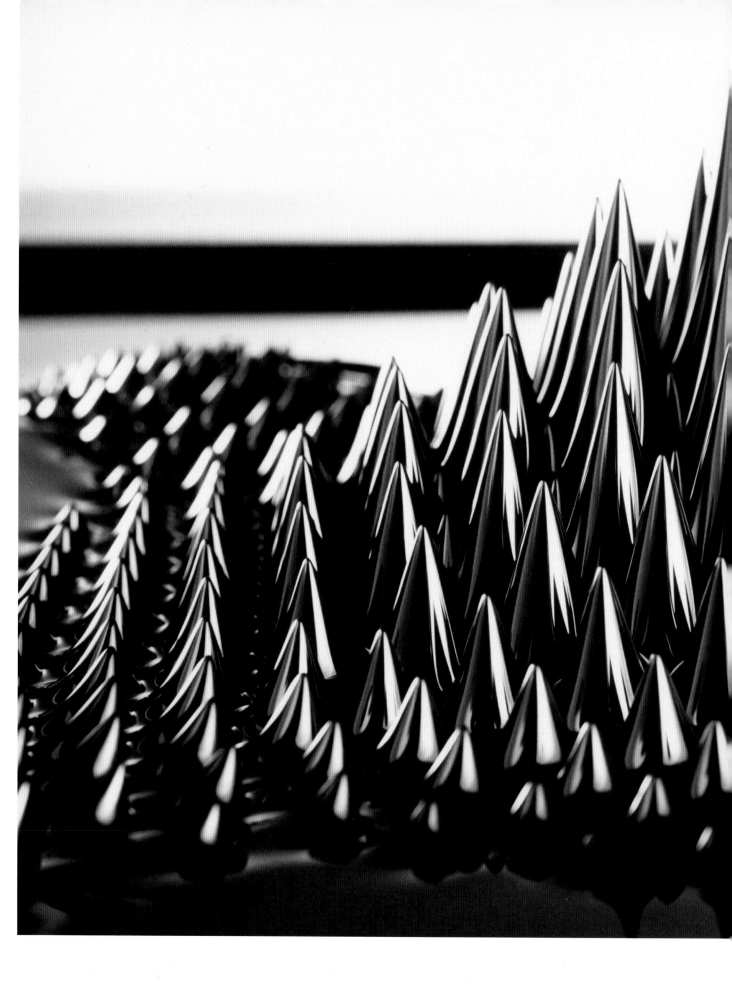

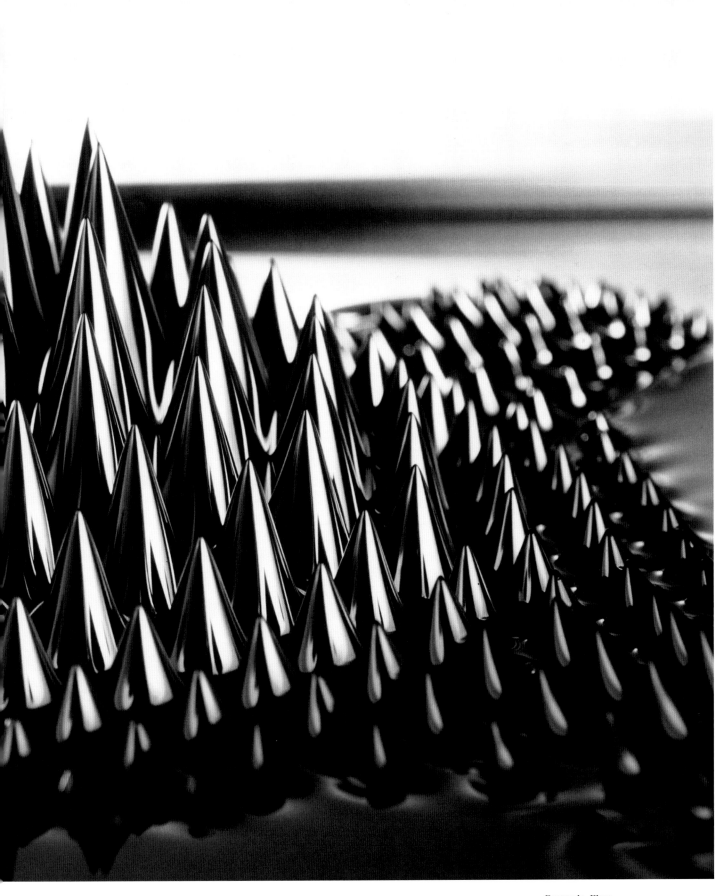

Protrude, Flow
2001
In collaboration with Minako Takeno

TAMBOURIN
ANALOGUE ELECTRONIC
INSTRUMENT

CIRCULAR

STRUCTURE
ANALOGUE ELECTRONIC
SOUND SCULPTURE

DUO
ANALOGUE INTERACTIVE
SOUND SCULPTURE

PETER VOGEL

Peter Vogel is one of the early pioneers in the field
of electronic sculptures. Since the late 1960s, he
has explored the potential of technology and its
intersection with dance, musical composition and
visual art. Vogel's sculptures are delicate constructions
made from analogue electronic components such as
transistors, resistors, speakers, microphones or
LEDs and forming intricate spatial compositions,
audiovisual constellations where the sculpture itself
is the logic circuit.

Their integrated microphones and photocells allow
the musical sculptures to respond to shadows and
noises made by the viewers with patterns of lights
and sounds that echo those of early synthesizers.
The interaction creates an engaging experience
of seeing and hearing elaborate improvisations,
which are unique, as the precise conditions of
their creation will never be identically reproduced.

But it is the quality of the compositions behind
Vogel's sculptures that make them such compelling
experiences. Vogel's sculptures musically share
a territory that is enriched by interaction and its
essential unpredictability, sitting with that of Detroit
Techno, Philip Glass and Steve Reich, in which
variations and increasing complexity result from the
addition or negation of repetitive phrases, a musical
language Vogel has developed and matured over the
forty years of his artistic career.

Tambourin
2000

Three mallets, photo cell, circuits, iron wire
84 x 20 x 20 cm (33 x 8 x 8 in.)

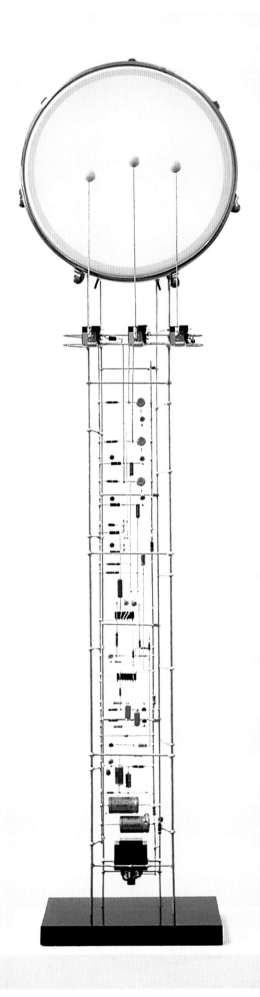

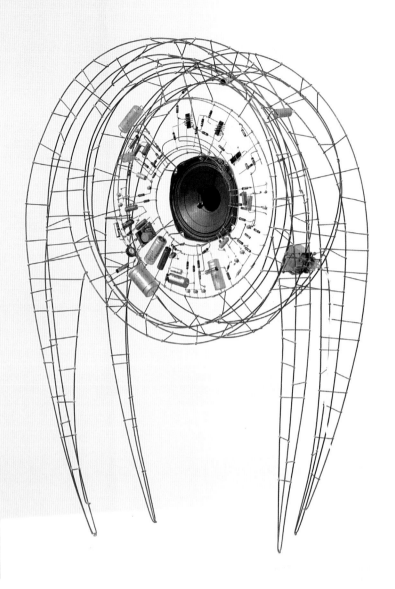

[left]
Circular Structure
1979

Speaker, photo cell, circuits,
iron wire
9 x 45 x 18 cm (3 x 18 x 7 in.)

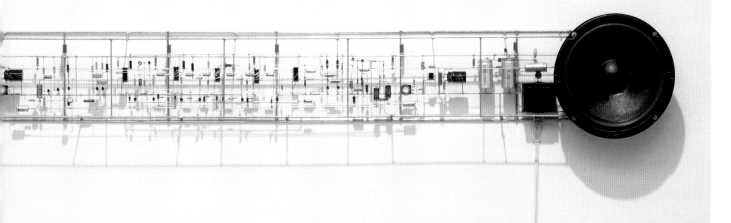

Duo
2006

Two speakers, photo cell, circuits,
iron wire
17 x 120 x 8 cm (7 x 47 x 3 in)

TOOL'S LIFE
MINIM++

Tool's Life is a poetic installation that explores and
stages childlike fantasies about hypothetical hidden
lives of objects. On a large, round table, lit with
a dim, white light that suggests the atmosphere of a
house at midnight in the moonlight, is set a collection
of tools, utensils and pieces of cutlery, placed in a
surreal upright position, with their shadows darkly
cast on to the tablecloth. If one slightly touches an
object, its shadow morphs and transforms itself,
thereby revealing in this dreamlike setting the true
nature of the artefact, the spirit within the object.
Suddenly, the shadow of the ashtray becomes a lizard
and runs away, the cake slice reveals and flaps its
wings, or the fork's prongs grow like branches.
Like many other works by Minim++, Tool's Life
transports us into a supernatural world, marked by
the animist conceptions central to Japanese Shinto
and reminiscent of Hayao Miyazaki's famous
animation films.

Tool's Life
2001
Interactive installation

Wood, metallic tools, touch sensor,
projector, computer
50 x 120 × 120 cm (20 x 47 x 47 in.)

THE SOURCE
MOVING PIXEL INSTALLATION
GREYWORLD

Created by artist group Greyworld, The Source is
a stunning interactive sculpture commissioned by
the London Stock Exchange for their atrium space.
The Source consists of a grid of 162 cables arranged
in a square formation and reaching eight storeys into
the roof of the atrium. Mounted on each of the cables
are nine computer-controlled spheres, which each
conceal a small, internal motor, allowing them to
move up and down independently along the length
of the cable. The spheres act as animated pixels,
modelling shapes in three dimensions, appearing
and dissolving away in a striking interplay of
particles rising and falling. Sometimes the shapes
are in an abstract arrangement, and composed
kinetically, while at other times the names and
positions of currently traded stocks appear.
The Source is thus a living reflection of market
forces: complex and sophisticated, fixed and
ephemeral, solid and fluid. As well as creating this
complicated sculpture within the space of six
months, with all the technical skill required to make
and control 1,458 individual, self-powered spheres
on cables, Greyworld have also, in The Source,
shown a perfect conceptual understanding of both
the context and its audience. The sculpture is typical
of their novel, playful and interactive approach,
evolved and perfected over the past ten years.

The Source
2004

COUNTER VOID
DIGITAL
COUNTDOWNS
TATSUO MIYAJIMA

Counter Void is pure digital poetry. Situated in the
busy, upmarket district of Roppongi Hills in Tokyo,
the installation consists of a giant illuminated glass
wall, more than 5 metres (16 feet 5 inches) high and
53 metres (173 feet 11 inches) long, covering a large
portion of the TV Asahi building. Inside the wall are
six large, digital counters, which endlessly count
down from 9 to 1. '0' is omitted: the counters mark
only a short pause before starting the countdown
from 9 again. As a metaphor of the cycles of life and
death, Counter Void manages to convey, by the very
simple method of counting, complex feelings and
profound conceptions about time, deeply rooted
within the Buddhist philosophy. The sharp contrast
between the deep blackness of the LCD ciphers
and the uniform brightness of the neon backlight
further accentuate the metaphor, while successfully
managing to create an atmosphere of peace and
contemplation among the installation's frenetic
surroundings. The anticipation of the final '0' and its
surprising absence create a theatrical moment that
acts as a clue to the deeper meaning of the piece.
During the day, the balance of black and white
reverses and the digits glow in an illuminated white.
Such attention to detail and the ability to knit complex
narratives into simple settings are typical of the work
of Tatsuo Miyajima, whose work, since the late 1980s,
has consistently used counting as the vehicle of his
artistic expression.

Counter Void
2003
Headquarters, TV Asahi, Tokyo, Japan

White neon, film glass, aluminium,
electric wire, IC time control program
5.1 x 53.9 m (16 ft 9 in. x 17 ft 8 in.)

FIREBIRDS
PAUL DEMARINIS

AN INSTALLATION USING
VICTORIAN TECHNOLOGY

The work of Paul DeMarinis often examines the complex interplays between meaning and materiality in communication technology, outside the official notions and sanctioned parameters of utility, efficiency or consumer desirability. He aims to question how particular material devices weave their way into personal relationships, social structures and our understanding of the world. DeMarinis often uses orphaned technologies, such as the one employed in Firebirds, to make apparent the impact of the materiality of technology on the meaning it communicates.

Firebirds is an installation consisting of a series of bird cages, in which a flame of acetylene and oxygen burns vividly. As if by magic, the flame seems to start speaking, transmitting into the air the voices of Joseph Stalin, Benito Mussolini, Franklin D. Roosevelt and Adolf Hilter, as recorded in the years 1935–36. The device is based on the principle of flame amplification, in which the flame itself becomes a powerful speaker as its plasma (the part of the gas that becomes ionized when heated) is seeded with potassium ions (from kitchen salt) and subjected to a strong electric signal sent through electrodes set into the flame. As the gas heats up and expands, it sets the air surrounding the flame in movement and creates the sound. This technology is of particular historical interest, as its discovery in 1904 led to the creation of the vacuum tube, a component that enabled the mass diffusion of radio.

The radio became massively pervasive on the domestic front around the 1930s, bringing with it, for the first time, the voices of our political leaders and thus politicizing our homes. With Firebirds, DeMarinis examines the complex power relationships between fire, language and communication technology from technical, historical and metaphorical viewpoints, generating an engaging experience of extreme complexity and intricacy, which powerfully questions and amazes, revealing the double edge of communication technology.

Firebirds
2004

CLOUD
DIGITAL FLIP-DOTS SCULPTURE
TROIKA

Cloud is a 5-metre digital sculpture, suspended in
the entrance atrium of the new British Airways
luxury lounges in London's Heathrow Terminal 5.
The surface of the sculpture is covered with around
5,000 small electromechanical indicators, flip-dots
that can audibly flick between a black and a mirrored
silver side, and which were originally used in the
1970s and 1980s to create signs in train stations and
airports. On Cloud, a sophisticated system controls
the flip-dots, which produce waves that chase across
the entire sculpture. Reflecting its surrounding
colours, the dense, mechanical mass is transformed
into an organic form that appears to come alive,
shimmering and flirting with the onlookers who pass
by from both above and below.

Cloud was created as a signature piece that would
mark the entrance to British Airways's new lounges
while also signifying the transition between their
calm and exclusive atmosphere to the business of
the shopping floor below. The designers started to
work on the metaphor of clouds to represent flight
and the contrast between the usually hectic airport
experience and the calm, luminous and ethereal
world that we discover as we fly through the cloud
layer. Further inspiration came from the materiality
of the flip-dots themselves, the noise they emit –
which is instantly reminiscent of travel – and the
time they take physically to rotate, altering the
reflections on their surface. The designers decided to
apply this redundant technology to create a sculpture
that was a sort of living organism. As the flip-dots
flick from one side to the other, viewers are instantly
reminded of rippling water, of the hypnotizing
movements of snakes and schools of fishes.

Cloud
2008
Digital sculpture

1 x 2 x 5 m (17 ft 8 in. x 6 ft 6 in. x 16 ft 5 in.)
Atrium outside entrance to the British
Airways First and Concorde Galleries
Lounges, Heathrow, Terminal 5, London

[left]
in progress
at Mike Smith Studio, London

3/GUERRILLA ARTFARE DISRUPTION AND HARDWARE HACKING

Guerrilla Artfare showcases grass-roots artists and designers who use and abuse technology and mass-produced devices, transforming and re-appropriating them into meaningful, surprising and inspiring experiences and objects. This approach concentrates on recombining, tweaking, tinkering and hacking. It is a source of fluid innovations, political gadgets and artistic devices to be promulgated as 'device art' or as real alternative products: quirky, inventive and refreshing reactions to the bluntness of commercial electronics.

BLACKMORE/ 180 ZACH DEBORD & KIM JACKSON DEBORD/ 182 BRIAN DUFFY/ 186 ROGER IBARS/ 190 SCHULZE & WEBB/ 192 OWL PROJECT/ 194 HULGER/ 196 SCIENCE & SONS/ 200 INDUSTRIAL FACILITY/ 202 MARK HAUENSTEIN/ 204 LUCKYBITE/ 208 RYOTA KUWAKUBO/ 210 TROIKA/ 212

GRAFFITIWRITER STREETWRITER INSTITUTE FOR APPLIED AUTONOMY

GRAFFITI MACHINES

Founded in 1998, the Institute for Applied Autonomy is an anonymous collective of artists, activists and engineers interested in the intersection between technology, public policy and social control, and the related issues of surveillance, public space and law enforcement. In a mock-official tone that reflects their genuine but often humorous attitude, their mission statement describes IAA as 'a technological research and development organization dedicated to the cause of individual and collective self-determination [...] providing technologies which extend the autonomy of human activists'.

The mission was fulfilled with their first device, the GraffitiWriter, a small, remote-controlled vehicle equipped with a series of computer-controlled spray cans on its back, which can paint propaganda messages on the ground as it goes. The printing process is similar to that of a dot matrix printer. GraffitiWriter can to be deployed in any highly controlled environment, such as shopping malls and government building complexes, operating at a maximum speed of 15 km/h and below the line of sight, disseminating unsanctioned content in highly strategic places. If authority reacts to it, the user, being at a distance, remains safe. IAA states: 'In repeated testing, this system has proven its effectiveness on such high-risk/high-profile targets as the US Capitol Building, as well as numerous urban commercial and municipal spaces in the US and abroad.'

The system was further developed in StreetWriter, a blown-up, wider, camouflaged version of the GraffitiWriter. It consists of a custom-built, computer-controlled industrial spray-painting unit built into an ordinary white van. It can print text messages several hundreds metres long and simple graphics that are legible from tall buildings and even low-flying aircraft.

«STUDIES HAVE SHOWN THAT IN NEARLY 100% OF THE CASES, A GIVEN AGENT OF THE PUBLIC WILL WILLINGLY PARTICIPATE IN HIGH-PROFILE ACTS OF VANDALISM, GIVEN THE OPPORTUNITY TO DO SO VIA MEDIATED TELE-ROBOTIC TECHNOLOGY.» AA RESEARCH DIVISION

GraffitiWriter
1998
Karlsruhe, Germany

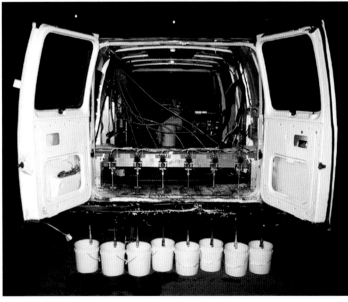

[above, left, opposite top, opposite middle]
StreetWriter
2001

The expanded width of StreetWriter allows for messages and simple graphics that are legible from tall buildings and low-flying aircraft and is capable of rendering messages that are hundreds of metres in length. The latest version of StreetWriter is called SWX.

[opposite bottom]
SWX
2004

LED THROWIES
LIGHT GRAFFITI
L.A.S.E.R. Tag
LARGE-SCALE
GRAFFITI
GRAFFITI
RESEARCH LAB

Originally founded by graffiti writers Q-Branch and Fi5e, the 12 artists of Graffiti Research Lab explore how technology can contribute to street art and urban communication and empower individuals creatively to alter and reclaim their surroundings. The lab has an open-source philosophy, and so each tool or technique it develops is carefully documented with a set of DIY instructions, freely available for download.

One of the first GRL inventions was a small guerrilla device called Throwie, which consists of an ordinary LED taped together with a button battery and a small magnet. The result is a tiny light that can be thrown and which will stick to most metallic surfaces. If arranged in groups, bigger graffiti can be formed, and the cluster will shine by night for up to two weeks. The artists have also created a kind of magnetic stencil, called the Night Writer, which resembles a long-handled broom with a steel plate on the end and enables a pre-arranged cluster of Throwies to be transfered to any outdoor steel wall cladding.

The latest offering from the lab is the stunning L.A.S.E.R. Tag, a system that allows individuals to write with light directly on buildings, displaying their personal communication on a very large scale. Comprising a powerful projector interfaced with a computer and a tracking camera, the system uses a small but powerful laser pointer as the user interface.

Holding the laser, the user draws on the building, the path formed by the laser point being followed in real time by the camera of the system, and the computer instantly generates a thick stroke of light projected back on the building. This results in an elegant and immediate interface, making for a witty and joyful experience. L.A.S.E.R. Tag is mounted on a tricycle, enabling easily deployment of the installation on to industrial facilities, monuments, towers, bridges and other hard and soft targets. The design and custom software have inspired enthusiasts to replicate the system in New York, Mexico City, Barcelona and Budapest. GRL also often gives public demonstrations of the system, inviting people to take the laser in their hand and have a go, creatively boosting their sense of ownership of the place.

LED Throwies
2006

L.A.S.E.R. Tag
(prototype)
Rotterdam, Netherlands, 2007

With James Powderly (US),
Evan Roth (US), Theo Watson (UK), DASK
(Berlin, Germany), FOXY LADY
(Rotterdam, Netherlands),
BENNETT4SENATE (US)

60 mw green laser, digital projector,
camera, custom GNU software

WILDLIFE
KAROLINA
SOBECKA

INTERACTIVE MOVING
PROJECTIONS

Karolina Sobecka is interested in exploring the intersection of motion graphics and technology, creating a range of interactive gallery installations and experimental films.

For Wildlife, Sobecka ventured outside the gallery context, putting the projector inside a moving car, and devised a system that allows the animations to be synchronized to the car's movement. At the same time, she created a series of wild animals that seem to run along with the car on the buildings' façades and respond to its speed: they run faster if the car speeds up and stop with the car at the traffic lights. The system is simple and ingenious: a rotational sensor picks up the speed of the wheels and controls the frame rate of the animation accordingly. Sobecka subsequently added another layer of interactivity in the form of proximity sensors: if the presence of a moving object such as a passer-by is detected, its animal avatar will also appear in the projection. Seeing a tiger apparently running along the streets is stunning and transports us into a world of fantasy. The system also breaks with the convention of static projections on to fixed screens and is strangely reminiscent of Dziga Vertov's experiments in his 1929 film The Man with a Movie Camera, for which he was the first to put a cine camera on a horse cart, thereby inventing the dolly shot.

TV-B-GONE
KEY-RING DEVICE WHICH
SWITCHES OFF ANY TV

MITCH ALTMAN

The idea for TV-B-Gone initially came to Mitch
Altman while he was sitting with friends in a Chinese
restaurant, where the noise of the TV was a constant
distraction. His annoyance spurred him into inventing
a product that will allow you to switch off a TV set
whenever you need to. In 2004, TV-B-Gone was
launched as a mass-produced device, a one-button,
universal remote control that spits out in sequence
every power code for every TV set around. Operating
the device is as straightforward as can be: you simply
point it at the TV you want to switch off, press the
button and wait for the device to send the correct 'off'
command. It was an instant success. Not three weeks
after the initial launch, the first batch was sold out,
and press reports were coming in from all over the
world. For a guerrilla enterprise that literally started
in a garden shed, without any initial investment, and
which developed mainly from volunteering work
from friends, it has morphed into a successful small
business – which demonstrates the need for more
risky, alternative products.

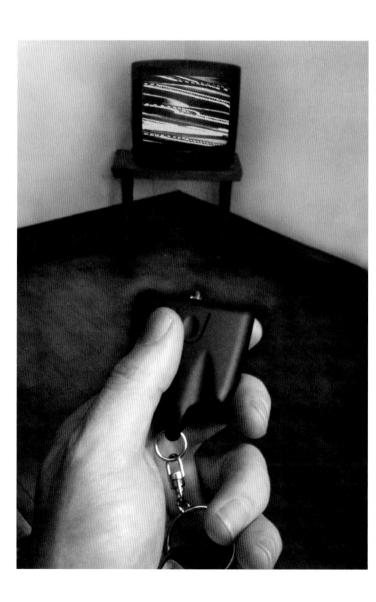

TV-B-Gone
2004

SPOKEPOV
LIMOR FRIED

MINIMAL INTERACTIVE
IN-WHEEL BIKE DISPLAY

Limor Fried graduated in electrical engineering from the MIT Media Lab's Computing Culture Group, which explores the social impact of digital technology. Reacting to the invasiveness of modern digital artefacts, she developed for a graduation project two counter-technologies to help people defend their personal space against unwanted electronic intrusion. The first device, called media-sensitive glasses, is an ordinary-looking pair of sunshades that will automatically darken when a television is within view, thereby shielding the wearer from the unwanted and distracting presence of the screens. The second device is a more straightforward mobile-phone jammer, which prevents the mobile from working within a radius of 20 metres. The device is small, portable and highly effective. Fried puts all the specifications on her website, so that you can make all the devices yourself if you wish.

This DIY approach is a constant feature of Fried's work. She has opened an internet shop to share knowledge about her inventions, as well as selling pre-made kits to a wider public. On her website you can buy the SpokePOV. Made with a simple controller, which monitors how fast the wheel is spinning, and a strip of 32 LEDs, this ingenious product makes use of the phenomenon called persistence of vision to create a floating, animated picture inside your bicycle wheels. The animations can be programmed to allow you to create your own manifestos, which you can disseminate in an eco-friendly way, simply by cycling.

TAPIS VOLANT
HEHE

Founded in Paris by Helen Evans and Heiko Hansen, both graduates of the Royal College of Art in computer related design, Hehe is an artists' collective whose work aims to rethink the existing technological systems that surround us, namely transport, public advertising and pollution monitoring, to give them a new social and critical usage. They see the development of technology as a kind of fractal image, at the centre of which lies the original invention, surrounded by a cluster of later, increasingly marginal innovations. This cloud of recursive innovations prevents us from seeing the up-to-date potential of the original invention, thus fuelling endless successive refinements. By going back to the core invention and navigating freely through time, space and culture, Hehe believes it is possible to reinvent an older technology without accepting long-established conventions. For this they use an artistic process they call reverse cultural engineering: starting from the original concept of the invention, they re-imagine the design decisions that were at some point in history considered unfavourably, but that could be equally valid for tomorrow. It is a clever conceptual hybrid between détournement, re-appropriation and a sort of fantasy design archeology.

Train and Flying Carpet are early outcomes of such a method. Between urbanism, vehicle design and automation, Train explores the aesthetics of movement and travel. Inspired by the Paris railway track 'La Petite Ceinture', which ran along a busy ring road and ceased operation in 1934, Hehe drew on the origins of the railway to propose an individual perpetuated vehicle. The individual train raises questions about the reality and 'real fiction' of traffic, challenging the language and aesthetics of transport, particularly those that have become so ubiquitous and unquestioned. It has also a poignant nostalgic and poetic relevance, as the vehicle potentially reveals hidden and disaffected parts of a city. Train recalls Tarkovsky's 1980 movie Stalker, in which the three protagonists enter the forbidden 'Zone' after a long rail journey made on a self-powered rail trolley. Flying Carpet is another vehicle of the same series. Installed on the disused tramline running through the centre of Istanbul, it becomes a timeless transport design that exists only in the imaginary world of fiction, yet stimulates our thoughts on what transport is and could be.

[above]
Tapis Volant
2005

Wheels, battery, motor, switch, wood, foam, textile

Tapis Volant
2005

[top]
Saint Denis, France

[bottom]
Driving along Istiklal Avenue for
'Vehicles of Registration and Omniscient
Observational Mechanics workshop'
(VROOM) at 'Istanbul Fragmented'

EARWORM ASSAULT DEVICES PAINSTATION FURMINATOR FUR

DEVICES TO SPREAD EARWORMS

CLASSIC ARCADE GAME
WITH PHYSICAL FEEDBACK

ANALOGUE PINBALL WITH FIRST
PERSON SHOOTER PERSPECTIVE

Earworm Assault Devices
Weapons of Mass Distraction,
2005

[above]
AAV-1
Audio Attack Vehicle v.1,
2006

*The desert-dog among the earworm
propagation devices: earworms with a
duration up to 12 secs can be recorded
and fired, but this time everything can be
operated remotely with the multipurpose
helmet-remote-control. The low weight
and durable construction combined with
the high velocity of the vehicle make this
device ideally suited for surprise attacks
in all terrains. The deployable radius is
limited only by your imagination and the
field of vision.*

[above left]
AEWAR-12.1
Automatic Earworm Assault Rifle 12 in.

*The fully automatic earworm rifle is
especially designed for situations where
long-distance and high hit-rates are
demanded. The earworm is recorded
directly into the magazine, multiple
magazines allowing for quick change
of assault tactic. The built-in target-laser
and night-vision spotlight make aiming
easy even under bad visibility conditions.
An extendable butt (not pictured) enables
fatigue-free handling and the pressure-
chamber-speaker satisfies with high range
and precisely directed propagation.*

Based in Cologne and founded by Volker Morawe and
Tilman Reiff, Fur came to prominence in 2001 with
their now famous PainStation, an arcade gaming
machine that inflicts physical pain on unsuccessful
players. Fur's gaming machines explore alternative
interfaces and interactions, which go beyond the
solely visual navigation, manual control and single-
user isolation typical of commercial gaming systems.

Fur describe PainStation as a contemporary duelling
artefact. It comprises a box housing a horizontal
screen over which two players face each other.
The game is based on the classic arcade game Pong.
Players use their right hand to control the left–right
movements of their bat on the screen, while their left
hand must be kept on the machine's Pain Execution
Unit (PEU). Removing your hand from the PEU
breaks the circuit – game over. During play, if your
screen bat misses a ball, your left hand is punished
with heat, electric shocks or a quick whipping on the
back of the hand. PainStation transforms the simple
game of Pong into an incredibly engaging game by
rethinking the interface and introducing real,
physical feedback, the possibility of receiving and
inflicting pain introducing a potent motivational
element. Pictures of bruised and bleeding hands on

[above]
PainStation
Enhanced Duelling Artefact,
2001–5

[left]
Detail

Fur's website are the best testimonial of the addictive power of the machine.

Furminator, conceived in similar vein, is an analogue pinball machine that puts the player in a first-person perspective, rather like the popular 'shoot 'em up' video games. The player's head is stuck into the Furminator capsule, which is like a huge virtual-reality helmet, right behind the flipper fingers and only centimetres away from the ball. Sealed off from reality, the player experiences this mechatronic world at first hand, the sound and mechanical noises, the light effects and the absorbing perspective creating a highly immersive environment. The interaction with the machine itself, not limited to pushing buttons, further enhances the experience. The whole body can be used to move and tilt the pinball until the Furminator admonishes you to calm down. This machine is an alternative vision of immersive virtual worlds, offering the advantage of involving most of the player's senses. Although the player is totally safe – being protected by an acrylic screen – the physical nature of Furminator also challenges his sense of danger as the steel ball sometimes comes towards his head at high speed. This feeling, highly integrated into real-world games, is most often absent from computer games.

Fur's subversive, witty and unconditional approach to gaming is also manifested in their Earworm Assault Devices, a series of guerrilla toys created to propagate earworms. 'Earworm' is the term that describes a song or melody stuck in your head, and loops for a varying time span. The 'infected' person often repeats the sound involuntarily by singing, humming or whistling, eventually spreading the earworm like a virus. As a result, earworms can be powerful marketing tools, and used as such to carry promotional messages and advertise brands, from pop music and audiobranding to cell phone ringtones. Fur's weapons of mass distraction enable individuals or small groups to distribute their own earworms. Small pieces of highly infectious audio material can be recorded on to the devices and fired at single or multiple persons, eventually spreading your message out into the world. They come in different shapes and sizes and are affordable on small budgets.

Furminator
First-Person Pinball
2004

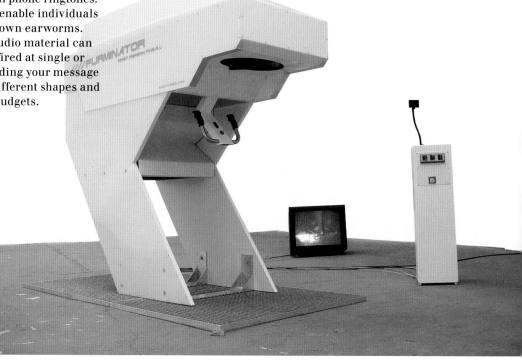

SHADOW
MONSTERS INTERACTIVE SHADOW PLAY PROJECTION
PHILIP
WORTHINGTON

In his work as an interactive designer, Phil Worthington puts a strong emphasis on the notions of play and playfulness, both as assets for the user's experience and as motivation for his own creative process. With Shadow Monsters, he revisits the traditional shadow play and explores how technology might contribute to create an even more compelling game. Through an elaborate interplay of computer graphics and camera recognition, the shadows cast by the users' hands are augmented to become the silhouettes of some strange and fantastic monsters, which react to our hands' movements with sound and animations. Form your hand in a C-shape, and teeth will appear in your shadow, with wild eyes protruding from the tops of your fingers. Now open your hand a bit and the monster will roar, burp and stick his tongue out. As the computer reacts directly to your hand patterns, there is no limit to the number and shapes of the monsters. Participants soon start to experiment with the shadows of their head or their elbow and legs, and begin to perform their monsters in this interactive theatre.

Shadow Monsters is, like many of Worthington's other works, a beautiful example of an open gaming system. It is a game with no precise rules, which, as Phil puts it, gives us 'a platform for experimentation and a space for the imagination to run wild'. It also shows how the technological layer actually adds to the magic and sensitivity of the original game, instead of becoming a mere distracting add-on. Shadow Monsters is hugely compelling, for both children and adults, as it visualizes something every child has once imagined when playing with shadows.

Shadow Monsters
2005

PIXELROLLER
COMPUTER-AIDED ROLLER
PAINTING TOOL

PIXELSHADE
LIGHT-PRINTING LAMPSHADE

PIXELOGRAPHY
PIXEL-
ROLLED
PHOTOGRAPHY

TPM EDITION
TEMPORARY PRINTING
MACHINE

RANDOM
INTERNATIONAL

rAndom International are 'thinkerers' in the purest
form. Their work concentrates on searching on the
fringes and within the leftovers of technology, art,
engineering and design, to create products and
experiences where the digital is embodied and
expressed in a tangible, analogue way. One such
product to make it out of the garden shed and directly
into the galleries is their digital painting machine
called PixelRoller, a performance tool designed to
paint computer graphics and text on walls and
ceilings. The machine is a sort of electromechanical,
handheld printer, which borrows the principle and
ergonomics of the traditional paint roller. The head
of PixelRoller conceals several smaller rollers,
controlled by computer to come into contact with the
wall or not, thus forming the image as the head is
rolled on the wall. The head is able to 'understand'
its position, allowing PixelRoller to be rolled freely
on the wall while still painting the correct image. It
is an extremely versatile device with a unique
aesthetic outcome.

rAndom have also developed a variation of this device,
working with ultra-bright UV LEDs on glow-in-the-
dark wallpaper. LightRoller works on the same
principle, producing a glowing image that has similar
graphic qualities to those of the PixelRoller, and fades
away with time as the medium releases the light
accumulated. For a series of photographs called
Pixelography, they used LightRoller on large
photographic papers to impress portraits, which were
then developed by the conventional dark room process.

Another spin on the idea is their beautiful PixelShade,
a large standing lamp whose shade, made of
glow-in-the-dark material, conceals a mechanical
arm impressing the phosphorescent medium as it
rotates by means of a series of UV LEDs placed at its
periphery. Unlike LightRoller, it works in an

PixelRoller
2005–7

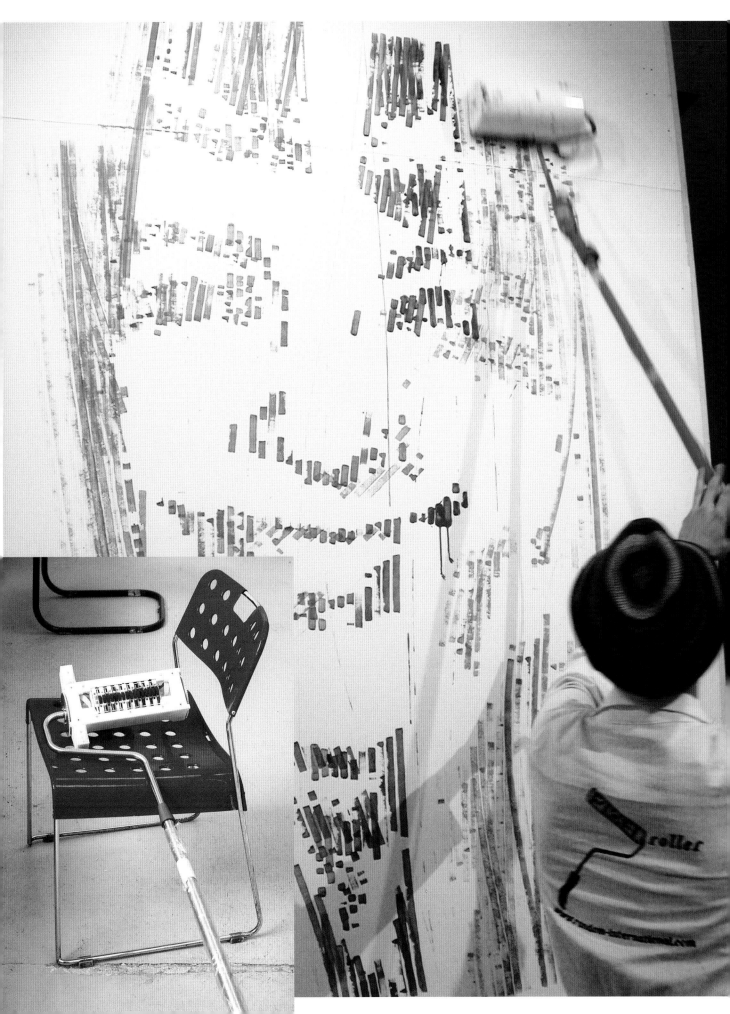

automatic way, allowing patterns and graphics to
appear and fade away cyclically.

Their later piece, Temporary Printing Machine, is
a large canvas-sized, vertical machine that uses a
similar system to PixelShade. A mechanical arm,
spanning the width of the canvas, moves cyclically
up and down imprinting a photosensitive ink
deposited on the canvas by a series of 192 UV LEDs.
The UV light will turn the invisible ink a deep purple
colour for about a minute, thereby enabling images
to appear and slowly fade before the machine starts
a new print.

[left]
Pixelography
2006
160 x 103 cm (63 x 40 in.)

[opposite]
PixelShade
2006

TPM Edition
Temporary Printing Machine
2007

«WE BELIEVE THAT A BETTER WORLD NEEDS A WORKING PROTOTYPE. WE BELIEVE IN THE MAKING OF PROGRESS AND ENGAGEMENT. WE BELIEVE THERE SHOULD BE POETRY IN THE MASS-PRODUCED OBJECT. WE BELIEVE THAT THE DIGITAL IS BEST EXPERIENCED IN TANGIBLE, ANALOGUE WAYS. WE BELIEVE THAT RAW SIMPLICITY COMMUNICATES COMPLEX IDEAS BEST. WE BELIEVE THERE IS AN URGENT NEED FOR CREATIVE TECHNOLOGY COMPETENCE. WE MAKE STUFF WORK, STUFF MAKES US WORK.» RANDOM INTERNATIONAL

SCANNER PHOTOGRAPHY MICHAEL GOLEMBEWSKI

HACKED FLATBED SCANNER
'STILLS' CAMERA

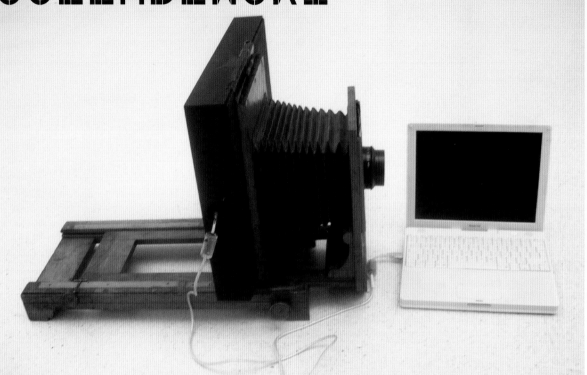

Recognizing that the tools we use to create art have a huge impact on how we express ourselves and how this expression manifests itself, Michael Golembewski chose to specialize in creating and developing new kinds of tools for artists, to open up new possibilities for artistic expression. One of Golembewski's most notable achievements is the development of an entirely new type of stills camera, based on an ordinary flatbed scanner. Golembewski made his first scanner camera while he was a student in interactive design at the Royal College of Art. He had the seemingly simple idea of taking a regular scanner and using it in place of photo paper with a large-format camera. When he started to experiment with his first homemade digital camera, he realized that wonderful things were happening in the pictures. Because of the scanner's slow scanning motion, the pictures produced would show clearly static objects, while every moving object would be subject to large distortions and appear to be morphed through space and time, rather like the effect created by moving a sheet on a photocopier mid-copy.

From a simple hardware hacking experiment, Golembewski had found a new tool for examining the relationship between time, motion and image. For the next three years, he will learn the language of the scanner–camera, to predict the results and learn how to expose or orient the scanner, constantly improving the hardware. This in-depth research has led to the stunning pictures featured here, which share some similarities with traditional photography while exhibiting others that are completely foreign, part analogue, part digital. The pictures exhibit a unique aesthetic as well as a warmth and randomness that would be difficult to achieve with imaging software or post-production. This experimental approach to photographic equipment, reminiscent of the wild creativity exhibited by the early pioneers of photography, is also welcome in a field that is largely dominated by a quest for high fidelity.

[opposite]
Scanner camera built
from an old magic lantern

[below]
Sonny Tufts Portrait
London
2006

Audi Series #13
London, UK
2005

City Bus #7
London
2005

HEKTOR
MINIMAL GRAFFITI-PAINTING ROBOT

RITA
ROBOTIC DRAWING MACHINE PLAYING WITH DRAWING SEQUENCES

JÜRG LEHNI

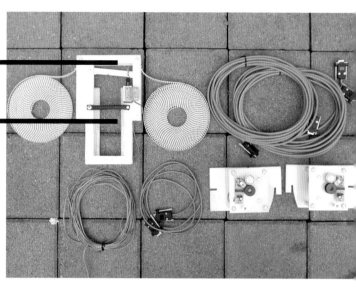

A result of the collaboration between engineer Uli Franke and artist Jürg Lehni, Hektor is a custom-made, portable, spray-paint output device for laptop computers. Created as a reaction to the ever-perfect aesthetics of commercial printers, Hektor consists only of two motors, a toothed belt and a spray can holder. The can holder is attached to the toothed belt, which, when subject to the pull-and-release of the motors, allows the spray can to be positioned as desired for painting. Custom software, starting from an original vector drawing, calculates the paths Hektor has to take and the correct rotations of the control motors. This results in an intricate series of movements, often de-correlated from the drawing itself, which creates a sense of anticipation and makes the device entertaining to watch. Small enough to fit in a suitcase, Hektor can easily be deployed to cover large areas with a distinctive, rough-and-ready aesthetic, complete with wobbly lines and paint drips.

A second machine, Rita, furthers Lehni's explorations into the performative qualities of drawing machines. A robotic arm that is able to record and reproduce line drawings endlessly, Rita erases them seconds after completion allowing for constant perfect reproduction of the drawing process but never produces anything as such, thus shifting attention to the narrative qualities of the drawing itself. Watching Rita is like watching an actual painter at work, but as there is a tension between the cold mechanical device and the warm human qualities of a real artist, the drawing is turned into something more abstract, a sequence of movements and forms. To enhance the ephemeral nature of the work, the inventor took great care about the materiality of the piece itself: Rita draws on semi-transparent glass, so that the process can be seen on both sides of the drawing surface.

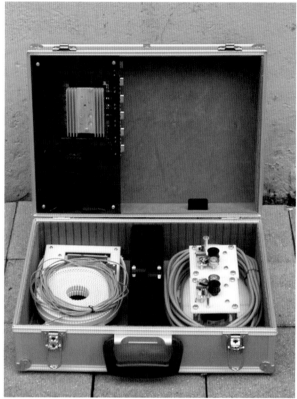

Hektor
Test #7 (Che)
2002

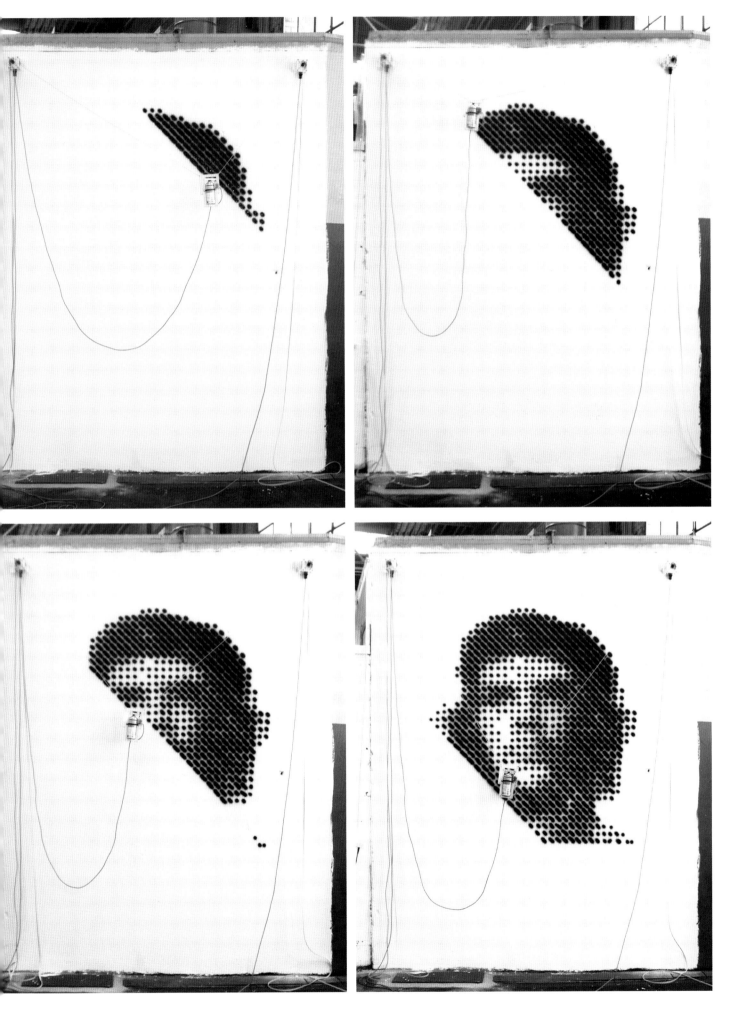

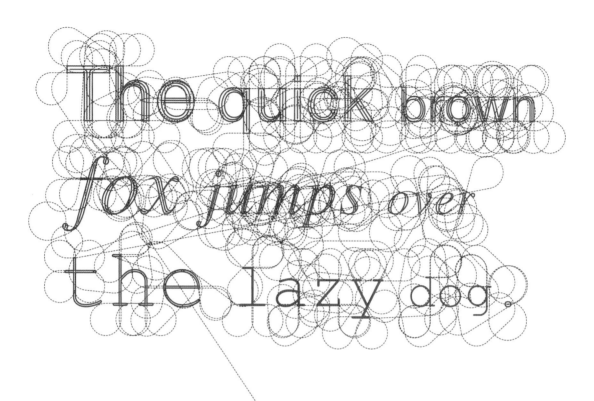

Hektor

[left]
Test #8 (Typography)
2002

[opposite]
Stay in Bed
First outdoor roof-top piece
Hektor & Alex Rich,
Fukuoka, Japan, 2006

Rita

[above]
Yves Netzhammer, digital drawing from
the series 'Die überraschende
Verschiebung der Sollbruchstelle eines
in optimalen Verhältnissen
ausgewachsenen Astes', 2003

[left]
Emma Åkerman, 'Girl with Fish on a Leaf'
2005

[opposite above and right]
Guy Meldem, 'It can only be attributable
to human error', 2005

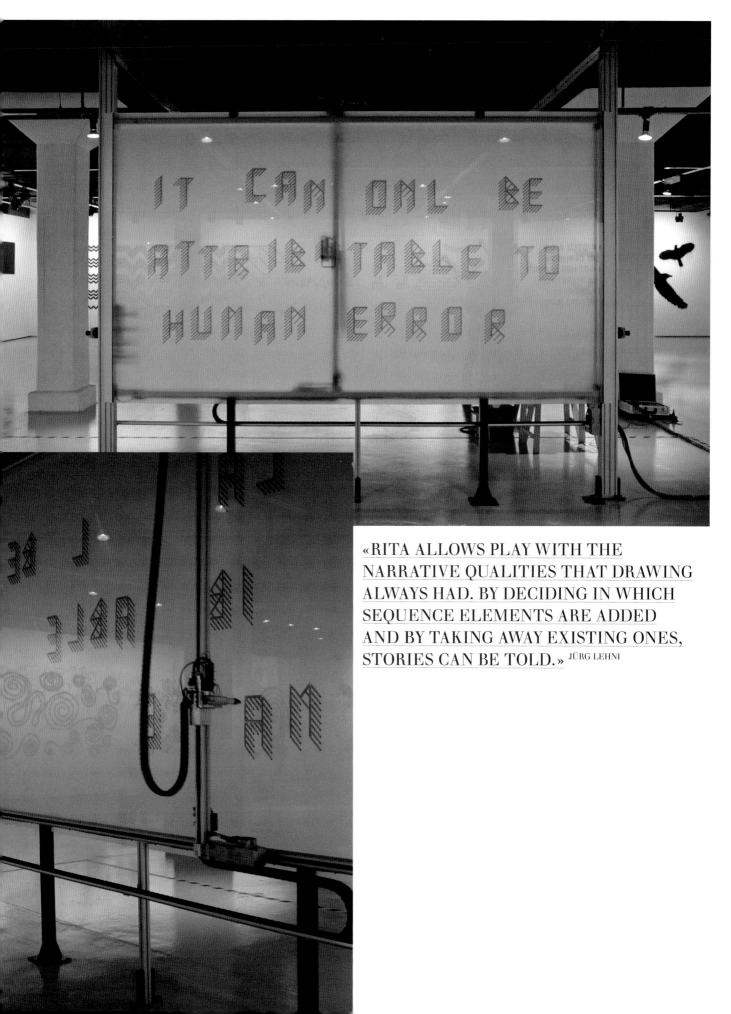

«RITA ALLOWS PLAY WITH THE NARRATIVE QUALITIES THAT DRAWING ALWAYS HAD. BY DECIDING IN WHICH SEQUENCE ELEMENTS ARE ADDED AND BY TAKING AWAY EXISTING ONES, STORIES CAN BE TOLD.» JÜRG LEHNI

WEATHER GUITAR
GUITAR PLAYED
BY THE WEATHER

SIMON BLACKMORE

<u>Weather Guitar</u> is a robotic guitar player that
responds to variations in weather conditions.
Developed by Simon Blackmore, this hacked
acoustic guitar draws parallels between the hard,
scientific inquiry of measuring and quantifying
the natural elements and the romantic notion of the
weather as a source of artistic inspiration. Several
sensors pick up the wind speed and direction, and
the electronic circuitry transforms this information
to instruct small motors to pluck the chords. During
the realization of this project, Blackmore has placed
special emphasis on keeping the level of programming
and electronics to a minimum, to allow the viewer
clearly to witness the way the systems work and the
influence of the weather in a direct, immediate way.

Weather Guitar
2005

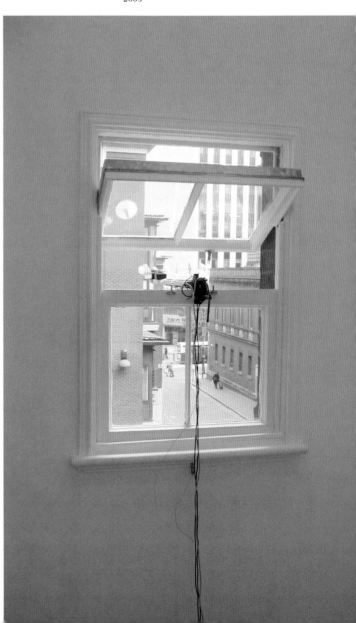

HELIOFORMS
ANALOGUE ELECTRONIC
BEAM ROBOTS

ZACH DEBORD &
KIM JACKSON
DEBORD

BEAM robotics primarily uses simple analogue
circuits without a microprocessor to create
surprisingly complex robotic behaviours. The
principles behind BEAM robotics, which stands
for Biology, Electronics, Aesthetics and Mechanics,
were established by robotic physicist Mark Tilden,
best known for designing robotic toys that include
the Raptor and the RoboSapien. BEAM robots are
beautiful examples of an alternative way of thinking
about robotics. The stunning, strikingly minimalist
examples shown here, made by Zach and Kim
Jackson DeBord, demonstrate an intimate
correlation between form and function. Starting
from simple analogue components – resistors,
capacitors, simple DC motors and transistors –
BEAM robots do not use any programming to
accomplish their tasks. Instead, behaviours will
emerge in the circuit, theoretically based on
mimicking biological neuronal systems (neural
networks). The results are usually simple in design
and highly efficient at performing their designated
task. Over the years, many scientists, BEAM
enthusiasts and artists have been developing
different typologies of BEAM robots, usually
classified by their behaviour. Phototropes are
robots that seek light, whereas audiotropes react
to sound. The robots usually have motors, which
allow them to move, and use solar panels as part
of the BEAM philosophy of creating autonomous
devices. Most basic forms of phototropes autonomously
seek and move to the brightest spot in a room.
Sometimes, elaborate BEAM robots will start to
express behavioural patterns for which they weren't
designed, such as always looking at the darkest part
of the room while being in the brightest spot.
This in turns consolidates the notion of a true
artificial intelligence – or perhaps our willingness
to believe in one.

Helioforms
2005–7

LEDs, mixed electronics, solar panel,
wire mesh, heat shrink and fabric
Varying dimensions, approx. 5–15 cm
(2–6 in.)

*Helioforms charge through solar energy
and perform a variety of tasks. Some
Helioforms roll or vibrate to move around
their environment while others simply
charge all day and pulse LEDs into the
night when they've detected it's dark
enough outside.*

[below]
*Vibrating Helioform triggers a small
motor to move around when it has stored
enough energy.*

[right]
*Three LED Helioform charges during
the day and pulses its lights when it
has detected it is dark enough outside.*

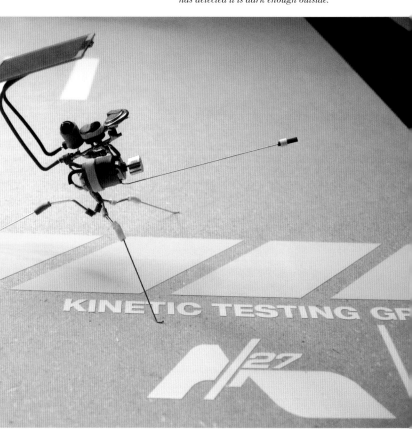

KINETIC TESTING GR

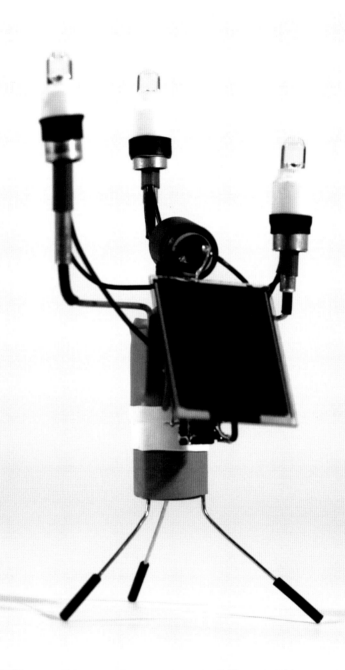

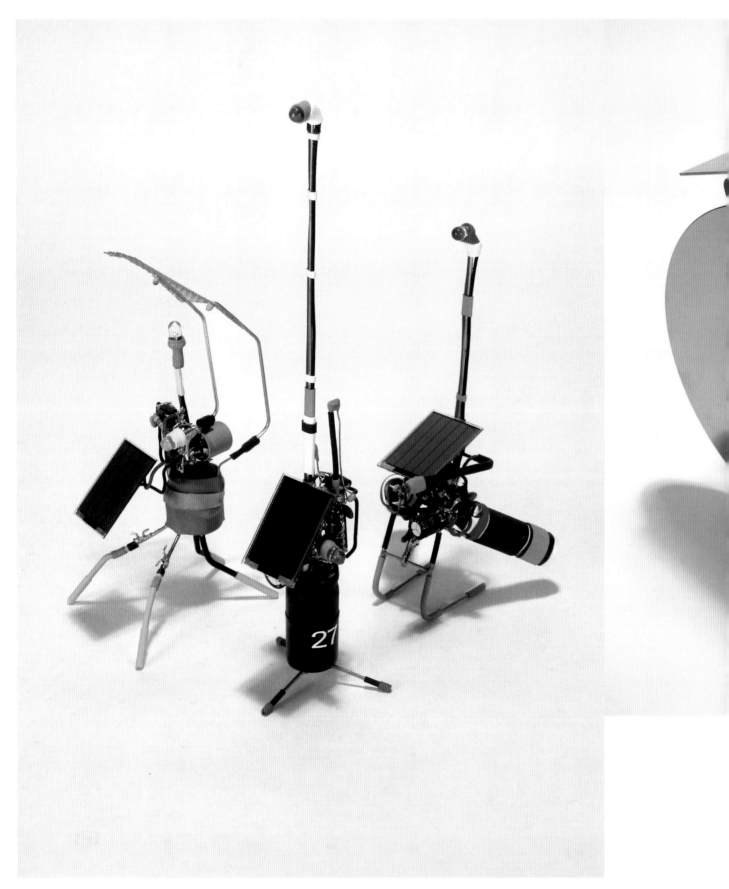

[above]
Variations of <u>Helioforms</u> that charge during the day and pulse their lights when they have detected it is dark enough outside.

[left]
Dual-engine solar roller follows the brightest source of light by alternately triggering each metal wheel.

[bottom left]
Phototropic Helioform *chases the brightest light source.*

[bottom right]
Light-seeking heading points towards the brightest light source.

MODIFIED TOY ORCHESTRA BRIAN DUFFY

CIRCUIT-BENT SOUND TOYS

Circuit bending is a playful and surprising form of hardware hacking, which emphasizes spontaneity and randomness. It consists in making creative short circuits on the electronics boards of low-voltage, electronic audio devices, such as sound toys, guitar effects or small synthesizers. By taking the toys apart and bridging different points of the circuit, this technique is able to reveal an amazing array of sounds, beyond those intended by their original creators. And by introducing additional components such as switches, potentiometers and capacitors or playing with skin resistance, circuit bending exposes the surplus sonic value of redundant technology and leads to the creation of strange and wonderfully sophisticated musical instruments. Circuit bending is believed to have been pioneered in 1966 by sound artist Reed Ghazala after a chance encounter with a transistor amplifier that would emit a stream of unusual sounds: the naked circuitry of the transistor was in fact shorted-out against a metal object in his drawer's desk. Since then, circuit bending has been at the core of a worldwide underground movement, which explores the hidden sonic (or video) potential of electronic gadgets, invoking 'the ghost in the machine'. Many sound artists and musicians have used bent instruments including the wonderfully quirky Modified Toy Orchestra, who uses bent toys such as Speak and Spell, small electronic drum machines and cheap musical dolls among others.

Sound artist Brian Duffy, master circuit bender and creator of the five-man Modified Toy Orchestra, is trying to break the familiar patterns made by traditional instruments and, by exploiting the unfamiliarity and randomness of bent toys, removing the ego from the composition process and getting away from the personal narrative, to concentrate on feeling, mood and emotion. He explains: 'You have to learn new playing techniques like skin resistance: touching brass contacts that connect directly to the circuits, the toys alter their pitch by drawing electricity off the circuit into your body. It varies with how hot or damp your skin is. These chance combinations add to the overall thrill of using the toys in a live performance context.'

Modified Toys
2001–4

[opposite]
Hula Barbie
Unknown Chinese manufacturer

[below]
PlaySkool Saxophone
Modifications of multiple touch-points

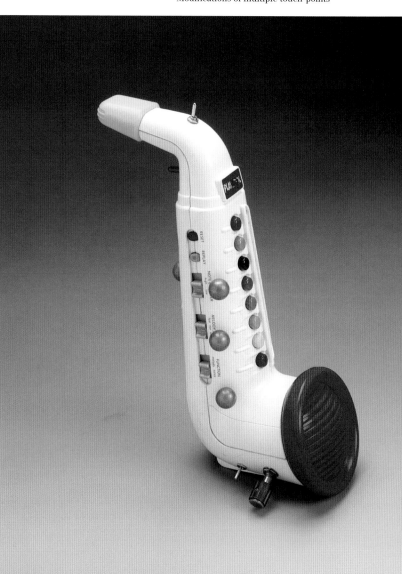

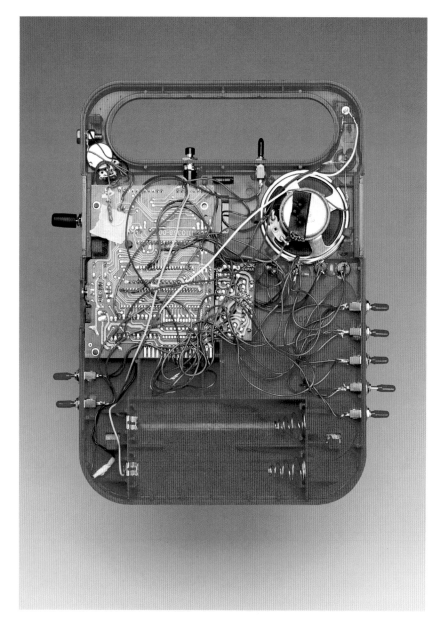

[left and below]
Speak and Spell
Texas Instruments

Front view and internal
modification detail

[opposite top]
Drum Kit
Happy Birthday Drum Machine

[opposite bottom]
Melotone Jazz Drum

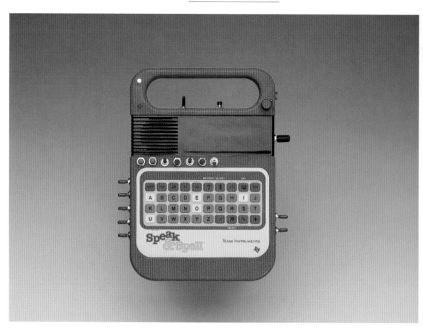

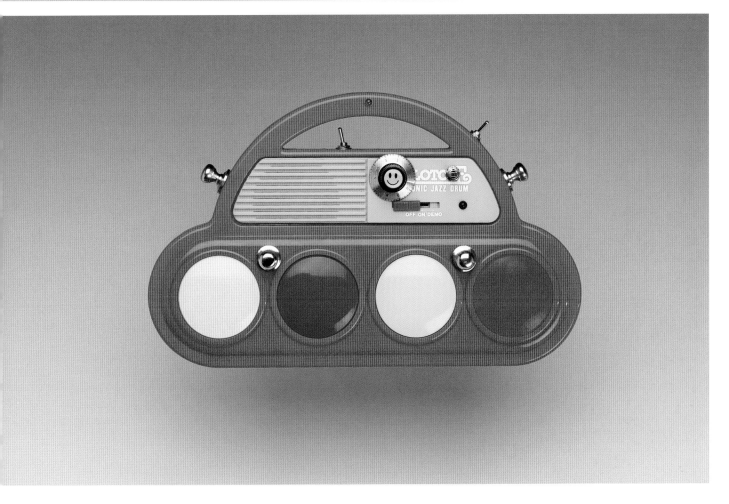

HARD-WIRED DEVICES
ROGER IBARS

HARDWARE-HACKED DEVICES

With his Hard-wired Devices, interaction designer Roger Ibars has taken hardware hacking – or physically disturbing electronic objects – to a new form: hardware remixing. Starting with his love for vintage electronic devices and the idea of exploring more playful interfaces for home appliances, Ibars began rewiring classic computer gaming interfaces to control more functional devices such as alarm clocks or radios. The results are playful objects that allow you to set the time or turn the alarm off using a joystick, a game pad or a light gun. Imagine shooting your alarm down in the morning; how satisfying would that be? On the conceptual level, the devices represent an interesting experiment in merging two completely different interaction cultures, that of home appliances – cold, functional and typically clear and immediate, with tiny buttons and minimal movements – and that of computer gaming – rich, physical, sensual, with many different possible combinations to be mastered.

[top]
Phaser Shoots Casio
2005

Hard-wired Devices:
Device: Light gun, Sega
Model#: 3050
Launched: 1986
Device: Travel Clock, Casio
Model#: DQ-560
Launched: 1980s
Hard-wired functionalities:
Turn gun 135° and fire: Alarm set up (h)
Turn gun 45° and fire: Alarm set up (min)
Turn gun 225° and fire: Time set up (h)
Turn gun -45° and fire: Time set up (min)
Hold gun: Alarm off

[opposite top left]
Atari Controls Philips
2004

Series: Control
40 x 60 x 12 cm (16 x 24 x 5 in.)

Hard-wired Devices:
Device: Joystick
Manufacturer: Atari
Model#: 2600
Model name: Standard Joystick
Launched: 1977
Device: Clock Radio
Manufacturer: Philips
Model#: 90 AS180/00
Launched: June 1978
Hard-wired functionalities:
Joystick forward: Fast time setting
Joystick backward: Slow time setting
Base button: Alarm set up
Half fire: Slow/fast setting

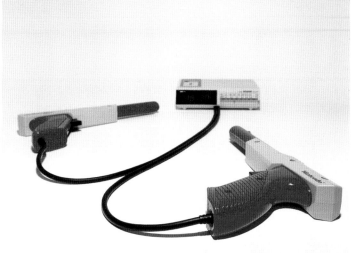

[above]
Nintendo Guns Shoot Philips
2003

Series: Control
Size: 5 x 80 x 50 cm (2 x 32 x 20 in.)

Hard-wired devices:
Device: Light gun, Nintendo
Model#: NES 005
Model name: Zapper
Launched: August 1985 EUA
Device: Clock Radio, Philips
Model#: D3142
Launched: March 1986
Hard-wired functionalities:
Left gun: Time set up
Right gun: Alarm set up
Full fire: Fast setting
Half fire: Slow/fast setting
Right gun fire: Alarm off

HARD-WIRED JOYSTICK FUNCTIONALITIES:
LEFT: TIME/HOURS SET UP
RIGHT: TIME/MINUTES SET UP
RIGHT + FIRE: ALARM/MINUTES SET UP
LEFT + FIRE: ALARM/HOURS SET UP
FORWARD: SLEEP ON
BACKWARD: ALARM/SLEEP OFF

Miami Vice
2005

Series: Control
11 x 35 x 60 cm (4 x 14 x 24 in.)

Hard-wired devices:
Device: Joystick, Mindscape
Model name: Powerplayers
Launched: 1988
Device: Clock Radio, Panasonic
Model#: RC60
Launched: 1980s

AVAILABOT
PRESENCE-AWARE TOY
FOR CHAT PROGRAMS

SCHULZE & WEBB

Availabot is a physical avatar that reveals the presence
of a particular friend on a computer network. It works
with instant messenger applications plugged and
plugs into the computer via a USB. When the friend
goes online, Availabot will stand to attention, only
to fall down when he or she goes away. Many of
them can be plugged in at the same time, thus
allowing the user to know who's online. As the
puppets are made in small numbers using rapid
prototyping for their external appearances, they
can be customized to look exactly like your friends.
Beyond the gadgetry of Availabot lie some interesting
thoughts about the nature of networked physical
objects. The puppets become tools that, in an
unconventional but immediate way, provide us
with clues about a remote situation, far extending
the boundaries of the screen.

Availabot
2006

ILOG
WOODEN ELECTRONIC
SOUND TOYS

OWL PROJECT

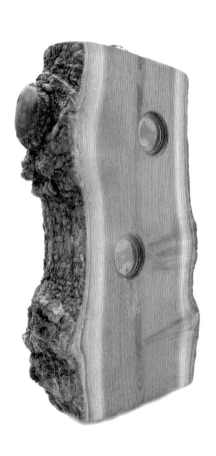

Active in sculpture and music, Owl Project are
possibly best known for their iLogs, small generative
electronic sound instruments retro-fitted into logs
of wood. Drawing their influences from both
woodworking and hobby-style electronics, Owl
conceived the iLogs as a reflection on our relationship
with consumer electronics. Although the name and
design of the objects echo well-known contemporary
products, their roughly crafted wooden housing
confers on them a traditional sensibility, which
the designers wanted to contrast with the disturbing
disposability of high-tech modern devices. If the
approach can be deemed nostalgic, it also leads to
a valid questioning of the physical homogeneity of
commercial devices, offering a beautifully quirky
alternative. Perhaps the most illustrative of the
critique is the iLog Rustle, which is meant to be
carried around everywhere and provide you with
music that is randomly generated through recorded
samples of your surroundings, which are then
transformed into beats, distorted and layered up.

iLog 005 Rustle
2007

Wood type: Laburnum

iLog 001
2006

Wood type: English oak

P*PHONE
PENELOPE*PHONE
PIP*PHONE

VINTAGE-STYLED PHONES FOR NEXT
GENERATION COMMUNICATION DEVICES

HULGER

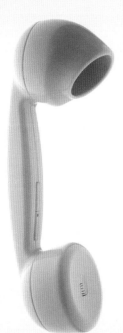

The concept for the Hulger handsets came out of a
reaction to the way technological evolution, especially
for mobile telephony, seems to be exclusively moving
forward, packing ever more functionality into an
ever smaller device. As Nicholas Roope, the founder
of Hulger, puts it, 'Technology always looks forwards,
never backwards. Why?' Nicholas started off by
collecting old telephones, rewiring the receiver parts
to use them as 'hands-full' kits with his mobile phone
and selling them as one-offs on eBay. But what started
as an artistic and fashionable pun on mobile telephony
soon began to resonate with people's feelings, and
Hulger's handsets began to attract attention from
both press and buyers worldwide. To cope with this
unexpected demand, Hulger formed as a company,
went to the Far East and started mass-manufacturing
their first product, the P*PHONE. New models have
since appeared, reflecting the same artistic vision of
a technology of simplicity, style and retro appeal, and
a line of products is now distributed in design shops
worldwide. Hulger has also started to branch out
into new territories, releasing a series of accessories
that enable the phones to be plugged directly into
computers, thereby creating a welcome physical
interface for internet telephony.

[above left]
PENELOPE*PHONE Bluetooth
Ivory
2005

[above]
PIP*PHONE Bluetooth
Yellow
2005

«WHY IS NEW ALWAYS BETTER? WHY IS SMALLER MORE DESIRABLE? WHY IS TECHNOLOGY SO SOULLESS? WHY SHOULD IT NOT BE FUN & BEAUTIFUL & INDIVIDUAL? WHY MUST IT ALWAYS LOOK FORWARDS, NEVER BACKWARDS?» HULGER

P*PHONE
Red
2003

Hulger's case is interesting, being one of the early instances
of designers bringing their product from idea to market
almost entirely on their own. As such, it is an inspiring
example of how an artistic device can become a real product
and many parallels could be drawn between Hulger's work
and Japanese device art theory. But, beyond the economic
model is the real appeal of the handsets, parasitic products
that make use of others devices' surplus functions to recall
a time when telephony was still a magical experience.

P*PHONE & USB*BASE
Red
2003

PHONOFONE II
IPOD GRAMOPHONE

SCIENCE & SONS

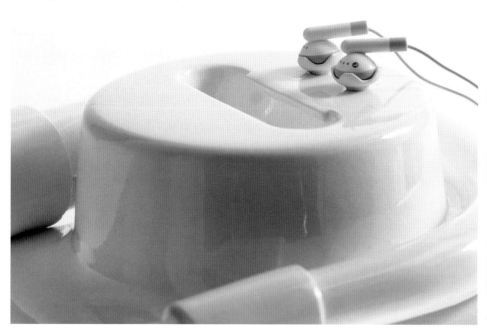

The Phonofone, designed by Tristan Zimmermann for his company Science & Sons, is a beautiful example of a symbiotic object, which, rather than being itself electronically based, feeds upon an electronic object to improve its function. The Phonofone instantly transforms a personal mp3 player with in-ears headphones into a sculptural audio console. Without the use of external power or batteries, the Phonofone amplifies the sound coming from the earphones to the volume level of standard small speaker systems, around 55 decibels. It works on the principle of passive horn amplification, identical to the old phonographs, except that here the exciters are the earphones instead of the needle vibrating in the grooves of the bakelite phonogram. The Phonofones are made in slip-cast ceramic, chosen for its stunning aesthetics, rigidity, low environmental impact and versatile production process, which enables low-volume fabrication of complex shapes without heavy initial investment.

Phonofone II
2007

Glazed ceramic
50 x 35 x 35 cm (20 x 14 x 14 in.)

PIXI

PARASITIC SOCIAL-NETWORKING
CAMERA

INDUSTRIAL
FACILITY

Pixi was created by Sam Hecht's Industrial
Facility in collaboration with Luckybite as a
concept digital camera specifically catering
for online social networking. It works with
the Japanese internet portal Mixi, an equivalent
of MySpace, where millions of Japanese share
their lives through diaries and photos. The
device is conceived as a simplified interface
for members to send photos automatically to
an online diary, a specific friend or a community.
Interestingly, Pixi is nearly entirely dependent
on the mobile phone that nests into it: the phone
provides Pixi with all the vital functions, namely
a LCD screen, a camera and lens and the internet
connection to upload the images. The ultimate
parasite, Pixi fulfils only one function through
its picture buttons, which act as shortcuts for the
locations images are to be sent to. Take a picture,
press the button and Pixi will automatically, via
Bluetooth, instruct the phone where to send it.
Customizable with stickers, the buttons will
also light up to indicate the online presence
of a particular friend. Although detractors may
regard Pixi as a mere gadget, an additional shell,
it represents an interesting way to address
problems usually associated with software
interfaces, and as such is a compelling device
that looks set to become a cult 'must-have'.
Moreover, the fact that Pixi instantly makes
you aware of an immediate audience can really
enrich your experience and transform the way
you take pictures and share them.

«IT WAS ONE OF THOSE NICE PROJECTS WHERE YOU KNOW YOU ARE GOING TO END UP BUILDING SOMETHING BUT THERE IS NO PRODUCT IN THE BEGINNING. WE TALKED A LOT ABOUT THE BLAND TYPES OF INTERACTION IN PRODUCTS, INVISIBLE SERVICES AND THE REALITIES OF FLEXIBLE DESIGN DEVELOPMENT WITHIN LARGE COMPANIES. A MAJOR PURPOSE OF THE PROJECT WAS TO USE A PRODUCT TO STIMULATE QUESTIONS.»
DURRELL BISHOP/LUCKYBITE

Pixi
2007
In collaboration with Luckybite
and Madori Kuroda

PANCAM TIME-BASED STILLS CAMERA
MARK HAUENSTEIN

Another parasitic object, which preys on the windows of moving vehicles, Pancam is a low-cost digital camera that records your journeys and fits them together to create infinitely long panoramic shots. Originally created by designer Mark Hauenstein, the Pancam can be affixed to any car window by two suckers. It works as a video camera, recording your entire journey. Once downloaded on to a computer, a custom application will automatically tile every frame of the video in sequence, delivering a continuous, extra-long photograph that can be printed on a roll of paper. The images make up a poignant memory of the journey, one that blurs boundaries of time and space, as well as giving visual clues to the pace of the journey. Pancam is a brilliant example of how the experience of something banal, like a small digital video camera, can be transformed by combining it with another object, here the moving vehicle. Paradoxically, the originality of the result comes from limiting the functions of the video camera, which is in a fixed position, instead of following the trend and expanding them.

[opposite]
Pancam
2005

[above and overleaf]
Panoramic images
taken with the Pancam

SKYWRITER

DRAWING TOY CONTROLLED
BY SATELLITE TV REMOTE

INTERNET
CONNECTED

CONNECTED USB DISPLAYS

DISPLAYS
LUCKYBITE

Product designers and innovators Durrell Bishop
and Tom Hulbert have long experience with
developing advanced technological devices and
interfaces. Their work is an inspiring mix between
commercial ventures for prestigious clients and
experimental projects, which often serve as test
platforms for new ideas, and which, following their
belief that electronic devices cannot be developed
solely on paper, are always prototyped to a working
stage, in a hands-on approach.

Their internet connected displays, for instance,
are a speculative type of interface developed while
the designers were employed by IDEO. They were
built to try out three different types of service, one
of which was a dedicated pair of displays that could
communicate only with each other, but from anywhere
on the internet. One person would write a message,
using a simple on-screen application, and the text
would be sent to the paired display, and appear as
scrolling to the other person. To stop the scrolling,
the reader would need simply to rock the display,
which would automatically send back an
acknowledgment to the sender.

Skywriter is a small drawing robot with a humorous
and ironic twist. For its control it uses the ubiquitous
Sky TV remote control (a satellite TV provider in the
UK). Press the navigation buttons to steer it, the red
button to record your actions and the green to repeat
the recording continuously.

Internet Connected Displays
2004

[above]
Skywriter
2006

VOMODER
MOVING FACE FOR PHONE
CONVERSATION

VIDEOBULB
AN ANIMATION IN A PLUG

DUPER/LOOPER
REACTIVE SOUND TOY

RYOTA KUWAKUBO

Japanese device artist Ryota Kuwakubo creates
electronic objects that mix interactivity with
humour. His first venture, a collaboration with
Japanese superstar artists Maywa Denki, is the
playful Bitman, a commercially available pendant
that incorporates a tiny electronic display on which
a pixelated character, the Bitman, moves and dances,
responding to gravity and shaking by virtue of an
integrated tilt sensor. The more you shake it, the
faster it dances and the more complex are its moves.
Turn it upside-down, and the Bitman will fall on its
head and collapse on the 'floor' before returning to
its dancing position.

Following the success of Bitman, Kuwakubo made
a series of small devices borrowing the same
aesthetic, of which VideoBulb is perhaps the closest
derivative. It is a brilliant device, a sort of USB key
but with an RCA plug, which allows it to be directly
plugged into the video socket of a TV set. It will then
show an animation done by artists with Kuwakubo's
bitHike software, a simple pixel animation program
that enables you to create Bitman-style loops.
Vomoder is another playful parasitic device that
plugs into the headset output of your mobile phone.
It analyses the voice of the person you are speaking
to and animates the mouth of the character on the
display, thereby acting as a kind of pseudo-video
phone. Duper/Looper is a musical object that behaves
like a drum machine. It has a little motorized hammer
and a shock sensor on its base. Placed on a table,
the device will copy and repeat the rhythmic patterns
that the user creates by knocking on the table.
To stop the drumming, simply grip the hammer.

[above]
Vomoder
2000

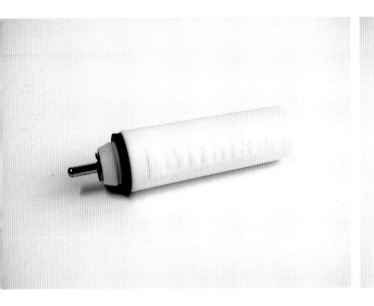

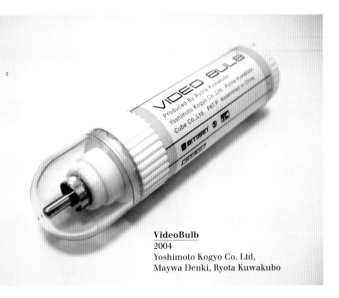

VideoBulb
2004
Yoshimoto Kogyo Co. Ltd,
Maywa Denki, Ryota Kuwakubo

[above left]
Original

[above right]
Product

Duper/Looper
2001

SMS GUERRILLA PROJECTOR TROIKA

PORTABLE TEXT MESSAGE
GRAFFITI TOOL

The SMS Guerrilla Projector is a homemade, fully functioning device that enables its user to receive and project text-based SMS messages in public spaces, in streets, on to people and cars or inside houses from street level. Small, portable and battery-operated, it integrates a mobile phone, which enables the device to receive messages emanating from other people, thereby becoming a tool for mass participation and allowing its users to display and share their reflections in an unexpected and versatile way. The device thus lends itself to numerous outdoor actions by night. Its unpredictability creates a special experience for people who witness it in action, inviting them to reflect on the content and implications of the messages. The SMS Guerrilla Projector is a good example of hardware hacking, as it is made by combining available technologies: a discarded black and white mobile phone, a vintage zoom lens for a still camera and the optics of a slide projector. It was created as one of a series of electronic devices with the theme 'subjective tools', which looked at creating functional devices for irrational desires. The SMS Guerrilla Projector emerged as a reaction to society's constant exposure to senseless corporate advertising messages and from the visceral need to create a media weapon that could re-appropriate this territory at grass-roots level.

[above]
SMS Guerrilla Projector
2003

[opposite]
'Where are we all going?'
Hammersmith, London
2007

4/TWILIGHT TECHNOLOGIES

CRITICAL DESIGN AND ALTERNATIVE FUTURES

Twilight Technologies explores the social, cultural and ethical
impacts of present and emerging technologies. The chapter is
concerned with works that show a decisively critical approach
and tackle the more complex, complicated issues of a highly
technologically mediated society. Here we see works that escape
pure functionalism to respond to social or psychological needs;
experimental objects and experiences that stimulate our thoughts
and connect with the darker pleasures and states of the human
mind, which conventional design often neglects; inventions that
are or that anticipate alternatives to the current technologies.

AUDIO TOOTH IMPLANT ISO-PHONE SOCIAL TELE-PRESENCE

MOBILE PHONE
TOOTH IMPLANT

SENSORY-DEPRIVATION
PHONE

TELE-PRESENCE
DEVICES

AUGER-LOIZEAU

The work of James Auger and Jimmy Loizeau
is a fine example of a critical design approach.
Their studio develops 'products and services that
contradict and question the current design ideology,
where development is mostly aimed towards a
super-efficient, multifunctional utopia for the
homogeneous user'.

One of their early achievements was a conceptual
product, originally proposed as a real one, which
was intended to spark discussion about the potential
impact of in-body technologies on society and
culture. The Audio Tooth is a radically new concept
in personal communication, consisting of a
miniature audio output device and mobile receiver
implanted in a tooth. The device transmits sound
vibrations through the jawbone straight into the
inner ear, making them clearly audible to the wearer
while people near by hear nothing. Audio Tooth is
a kind of electronic telepathy that opens up endless
possibilities: prime ministers receiving instant,
secret guidance from advisers, football coaches
giving tactical instructions to their players, traders
receiving financial information – and cheats winning
at card games....To increase their credibility when
they presented their device to the public and media,
Auger and Loizeau created a spoof company, Mibec
Corporation. The Audio Tooth taps into our
technological dreams and fears, veering between
the fantastic and the feasible. It has been greeted
with much interest all over the world, stimulating
discussion about the future of technology, while
demonstrating a successful and original way
to bring critical thinking into design outside
of galleries and academia.

Auger–Loizeau continued their exploration
of communication technologies with Social
Tele-Presence, in which the hardware connects

«INITIALLY PROPOSED AS A REAL PRODUCT, THE AUDIO TOOTH IMPLANT IN REALITY IS A CONCEPTUAL PROPOSITION INTENDED TO ENCOURAGE DISCOURSE AND COMMENT ON THE POSSIBILITIES OF IN-BODY TECHNOLOGY AND THEIR POTENTIAL IMPACT ON SOCIETY AND CULTURE.» AUGER–LOIZEAU

wirelessly a pair of stereo headsets and TV glasses
to a mobile camera fitted with binaural microphones.
The head movements of the wearer are monitored
and transmitted directly to the remote camera,
in real time, thus teleporting the visual and aural
senses of the user to another location and giving him
the opportunity to be instantly transported to remote
places, without moving. In this way, for example,
a disabled person could experience a walk in the
country by attaching the remote camera to the back
of a dog, or an armchair tourist could sightsee in a
remote city by logging in to a camera affixed to the
roof of a taxi. A more complex scenario could lead
to a kind of rent-a-body service, enabling the user
to send his own sensations to another person in a
different location. The physical avatar could enable
us to remotely attend meetings or satisfy our
voyeuristic impulses without repercussions.

Iso-Phone is another alternative communication
device, which creates a communication experience
of heightened intimacy and purity. It can best be
described as a cross between a telephone and a
flotation tank. The user wears a helmet that blocks
out all unnecessary sensory input, while keeping
his head above the surface of the water. The water
is heated to body temperature, thus removing bodily
sensations, inducing a meditative state in the user.
This forms a pure, distraction-free environment for
making a telephone call, the only sensory stimulus
being a two-way voice connection to someone using
the same apparatus in another location.

Iso-Phone
2003–4

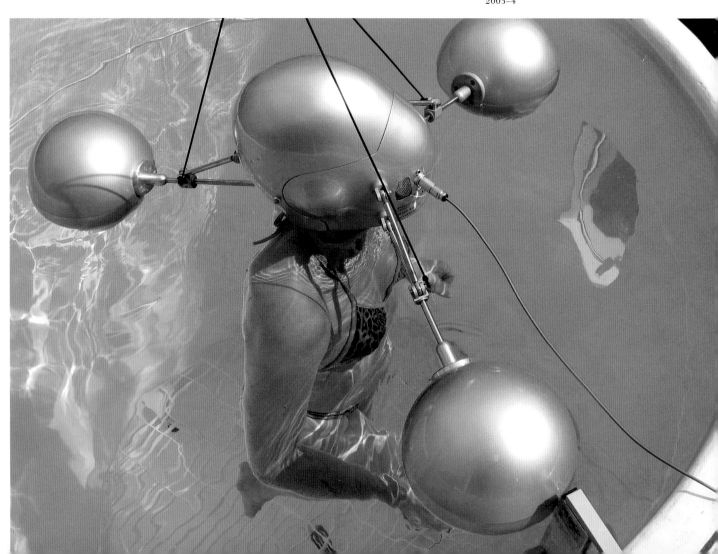

Social Tele-Presence
2001

[opposite and top]
In the same way that the eyes of a dog enable a blind person to see, their legs can be used to enable people to walk while remaining stationary. In this way the user can window-shop from home or take a walk in the country.

[above]
Through the rent-a-body service individuals of a nervous disposition or lacking social skills can use the rented body to go on blind dates in their place.

ACCESS
AN INSTALLATION DEALING WITH CONTROL AND CELEBRITY

MARIE SESTER

Picture yourself walking down an alleyway or strolling quietly in a shopping mall. Suddenly a spotlight singles you out of the crowd and follows you around: you are now the centre of attention. You hear a voice saying, 'You are being watched by 35,455 people now. Please entertain them.' Startled, you wonder who is tracking you? How? And why? In reality, you have been singled out by someone using the web interface of the installation, which shows a real-time video of the space and lets the user choose his victims. The software then controls a robotic track light, which follows you until you leave the detection zone. A directional speaker is also used to address you: you don't know this, but you are the only one hearing the voice. You become the artwork. How will you react? This is the basic plot of ACCESS, an installation created by media artist Marie Sester to explore the ambiguities in modern culture around surveillance, control,

visibility and celebrity. ACCESS sets the stage for an intentionally ambiguous situation, the person singled out being both the target of an elaborate surveillance system and an instant celebrity. The reactions of the audience reveal our fascination with these issues and the underlying perverseness of our media environment. Some individuals may not like the idea of being under surveillance. Some individuals may love the attention. That is part of the appeal of ACCESS.

[opposite]
ACCESS
Softopia Center, Ogaki, Gifu, Japan
2002

[top]
ACCESS
Ars Electronica, Linz, Austria
2003

[above left]
ACCESS
EYEBEAM, New York
2003

DESIRE
MANAGEMENT
DEVICES ADDRESSING
PSYCHOLOGICAL CONDITIONS
BRA REMOVAL
TRAINER
SOCIO-CULTURAL
COMMENTARY AS OBJECT
NOAM TORAN

Designer and filmmaker Noam Toran uses specifically designed objects and curated films to investigate the social, psychopathological implications of emerging technologies, mass culture and celluloid media, in an attempt to both define and criticize the intersection between science and society, modernity and culture. His products are developed for individuals as vehicles for self-expression and a celebration of the uniqueness of the self and of its intimate desires and fantasies.

Desire Management is a film that presents a series of specifically designed products attached to 'ab-normal' behaviours. In the film, which is based on real testimonials, the domestic space is defined as the last private frontier where alienated individuals can use these bespoke appliances to engage in unorthodox experiences, reflecting their inherent need for expression and identity formation in the face of conformity. An aeroplane trolley with built-in turbulence was made for a former airline hostess who suffered a panic attack on a flight, which led to her dismissal. The object is part of her therapy to regain confidence in the air: it has a built-in mechanism that replicates the effects of turbulence and has foot pedals to stand on.

Another example of Toran's work is the Bra Removal Trainer, a fictional teaching aid designed to instruct adolescent boys master the intricacies of opening the brassiere. The machine mechanically demonstrates the principles of undoing the clasp and removing the bra. Following a short pause the machine then re-secures the bra ready for the next demonstration. The project was originally inspired by accounts of repressive post-war institutionalised sex education, but is meant to serve as a future artifact, demonstrating an obsolete behaviour brought about by developments in bio-technology and plastic surgery.

Desire Management
2004–6

Running Time: 11 min 20 sec
Originating format: Super 16mm, HD
Festival screening format:
HD, Digibeta, Beta SP PAL
In collaboration with Director of
Photography Per Tingleff.

Turbulent Air Hostess Trolley

Sabena cabin trolley, aluminium,
motors, electronics, speakers

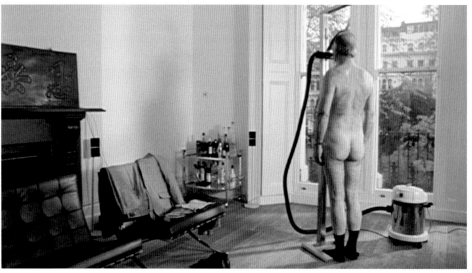

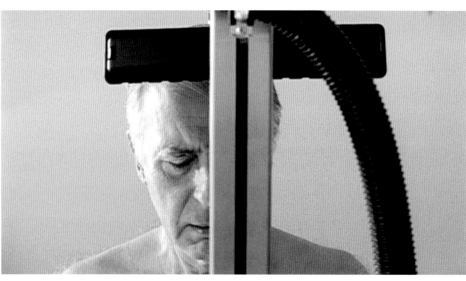

[above]
Baseball Bed

Plywood, artificial grass, leather belts,
baseball bag, earth, CD player, speakers

*A suitcase opens up to become a bed
shaped from a section of a baseball
field, specifically the third base bag and
foul area. The client is a 35-year-old
Japanese man who lost his virginity on
a baseball field and wishes to revisit the
experience with future partners.*

[left]
Vacuum Scanner

Vacuum cleaner, stainless steel,
electronics, motor

*Body-sized scanner with vacuum cleaner,
which can be used in both a vertical or
horizontal position. The client used to be
vacuumed by his wife as an end-of-the-
day relaxation ritual. She passed away
last year and he requested a vacuuming
machine that he could use by himself.*

Bra Removal Trainer
2007

In collaboration with Nick Williamson

Bra, custom electronics, machined
aluminium components, DC motor,
LED, powder-coated steel

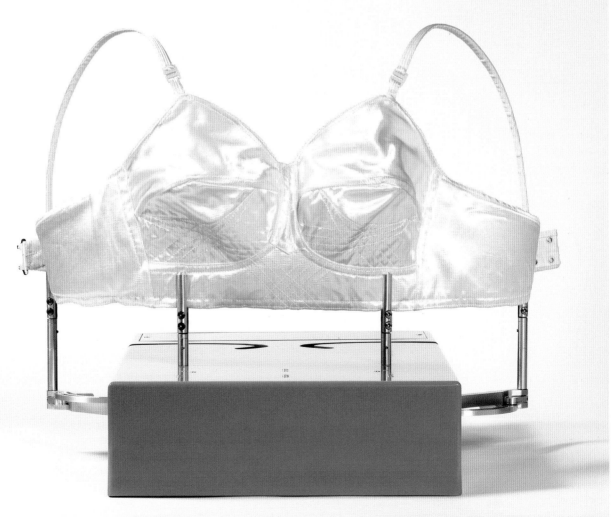

FERAL ROBOTIC DOGS

SOCIAL ROBOTS THAT DETECT POLLUTANTS

OOZ PROJECT

NOVEL INTERFACES IN HUMAN–ANIMAL COMMUNICATION

NATALIE JEREMIJENKO

Natalie Jeremijenko is an academic, scientist, artist and environmental activist. She develops installations that aim to explore the human/animal interface, to raise awareness about environmental issues – often considered at a systemic level – and to redefine the structures of participation in the environment and its population. Her Feral Robotic Dogs project investigates the more pragmatic roles robots can play on a social level by re-purposing pet/toy robots, fitting them, for instance, with environment toxin sensors. This enables the robots to spot invisible but dangerous pollution in landfills or in urban areas suspected of contamination, as the robots are able to follow concentration gradients of a particular toxin and with their movements visually display, in a readily accessible way, the measured information. In true activist spirit, the project is open so as to enable as many dogs as possible to be released on a particular site at any one time, thus creating a highly visual and mediagenic event, which draws attention to the contaminated site.

Ooz – 'zoo' spelt backwards – is a series of projects and experiments that explore interactions between humans and animals. Conceptually, Ooz is a place where animals remain by choice, a zoo without cages, representing a more engaged, reciprocal and respectful relationship with animals. Ooz incorporates a series of human–animal communication devices, such as the robotic geese, camouflaged, remote-control goose robots that enable participants to interact with actual birds in an urban context and come to understand and accept them better. The robots' interface allows people to approach the geese, follow them closely and interact with them: the robots can 'talk' to the geese using pre-recorded goose 'words', and are fitted with mics and video camera to stream what they see and hear back to the user.

In another Ooz project, Jeremijenko and her collaborator, architect Laura Kurgan, reverse-engineered documented techniques in order to prevent bats from occupying a building and roof. The purposely bat-friendly architecture incorporates a martini bar, where the bats, flying in and out at dusk, provide sound and visual entertainment for the drinkers.

[above]
Feral Robotic Dogs
2002

[left]
Robotic Geese
2003

TRIGGER
HAPPY RAPID-MANUFACTURED WEAPON
TIM STOLZENBURG

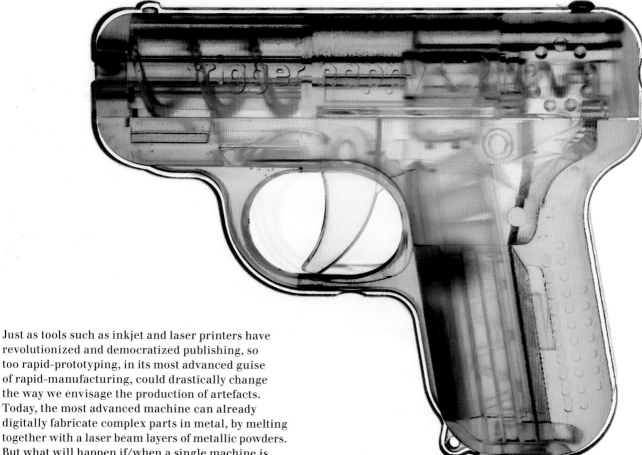

Just as tools such as inkjet and laser printers have revolutionized and democratized publishing, so too rapid-prototyping, in its most advanced guise of rapid-manufacturing, could drastically change the way we envisage the production of artefacts. Today, the most advanced machine can already digitally fabricate complex parts in metal, by melting together with a laser beam layers of metallic powders. But what will happen if/when a single machine is able, from a computer model, to fabricate the most intricate of products, from any material and without the need for further assembly? What will happen to industry when these machines can be purchased at low cost and become standard equipment in every household? What will then become the currency? Will it be the digital descriptions, the 'recipes' for the objects? What will people then choose to fabricate?

To invite us to reflect on the potential impacts of technology, designer Tim Stolzenburg has designed Trigger Happy, a rapid-prototyped gun – made with stereolithography – which could, with the advance in digital manufacturing, simply be downloaded from the internet and made as a fully working, enclosed system. But he also highlights the dangerous potential of the process, which allows for the uncontrolled creation of artefacts, for example a gun that carries no brand, marking or serial number.

Trigger Happy
Stereolithography gun
2005

SUBVERSIVE
SIGHTSEEING CATASTROPHIC TELESCOPE
TIM SIMPSON

Subversive Sightseeing is a site-specific public
installation set up on Hungerford Bridge, London,
in June 2006. It consists of a coin-operated telescope,
as commonly found at viewpoints. The device is
modified to show an alternative panorama, which
responds to the telescope's movements, but is actually
a film in which a sequence of epic catastrophes takes
place: in the distance a crane collapses, an atomic
mushroom cloud appears on the horizon and a
capsule on the London Eye dangles precariously
over the Thames. Of course, the telescope is placed
precisely where the real panorama and the one seen
through the device match.

Subversive Sightseeing plays with the receptivity
and awe we have, as tourists, for the scale and
permanence of the city landscape, surprising and
confusing our sense of reality and our trust in the
built architectural landscape. As Tim Simpson puts
it, 'The device is intended to recognize the cinematic
ingenuity of our fantasies, and the ramifications events
such as 9/11 have on our collective imaginations.'
As such, Subversive Sightseeing is a successful
example of a device with an intricately knitted
narrative content, which arouses emotions in
a similar way to film, while taking advantage of
the physicality of both the object and its context.

Subversive Sightseeing
2006

Coin-operated telescope, film

TECHNOLOGICAL DREAM SERIES: NO.1, ROBOTS DO YOU WANT TO REPLACE THE EXISTING 'NORMAL'?

FUTURE
BEHAVIOURAL
ROBOTS

DESIGNS FOR
IRRATIONAL NEEDS

DUNNE & RABY

Anthony Dunne and Fiona Raby are among the first designers to advocate a more critical and conceptual approach in design, to challenge our assumptions and preconceptions about the role products can play in our lives and societies, present or future, real or fictional. They use products and services as a medium to stimulate discussion and debate among designers, the industry and the public about the social, cultural and ethical implications of technology, existing and emerging. In this respect, their designs often look at the darker desires that fuel technological development, catastrophic scenarios and products for irrational impulses and needs, challenging and transcending the narrow corporate and utilitarian, commercial understanding of design. Proponents of the Critical Design movement, Dunne & Raby are the authors of several publications in which they express their design philosophy, perhaps the best known being *Design Noir: The secret life of electronic objects*, in which they take us into the darker world of electronics with stories about electromagnetic radiations, pirate broadcasting, automated alibi services and the like....

Technological Dreams Series: No. 1, Robots starts from the common assumption that one day robots will do everything for us. Invisible robots are already at work, controlling our everyday lives in our cars, offices and industries, but robots, in the form of androids, are one of the oldest and deepest-rooted technological dreams. Androids have had a place as

far back as in Greek mythology with Ephaistos, the blacksmith god, who created two maidens made of gold, to help him in his everyday tasks.

How, we wonder, will robots evolve in the years to come? Will they start to take on more and more human traits and behaviours, as their intelligence increases or their workings are increasingly based on more organic principles such as neuronal networks or biological power? How will we interact with them? To explore these questions, Dunne & Raby have created a series of robots of the future. Robot No. 1, shaped like a red ring, is a very powerful robot, which performs complex calculations to control our data-intensive smart homes and lives. It is discreet and independent, and although we may not know exactly what it does, the important thing is that it does it well. To do so, however, it needs to shield itself from strong electromagnetic fields generated by other objects such as mobile phones, and so it will always move to the most magnetically quiet part of the room. Because of its ring shape, its owner can, for example, place a chair in it, knowing that the spot is a good one. Future robots may not be designed with a specific task in mind. Instead, they may develop the specific qualities they need for a task assigned to them (see emerging behaviours of BEAM robots in section 3). One such is Robot No. 2, black in colour and fitted with multiple cameras to protect the security of a home. It is extremely paranoid and constantly scrutinizes the world

Technological Dream Series:
No. 1, Robots
2007

Robot No. 4

*This one is very needy. Although extremely
smart, it depends on its owner to move
it about. Originally, manufacturers
would have made robots speak human
languages, but over time they will evolve
their own language. You can still hear
human traces in its voice.*

around it, but is also shy, and rolls away when humans approach it. Robot No. 3 is a repository for personal information and will need to make sure you are its legitimate owner by scanning your irises. Robot No. 4 is the nerdy, needy one, having a powerful brain in an underdeveloped body, and needing to be wheeled around by its owner – a scenario in which robots partly take on human traits and imperfections. Robot No. 5 is an organic stomach robot, which derives its energy from an organic bacterial reactor, capable of digesting anything from slugs to rotting apples. Will the fact that we need to feed our robots change our relationship with them?

In another recent project with the explicit title Do You Want to Replace the Existing 'Normal'?, Dunne & Raby propose objects dealing with irrational, complex feelings and fixations. Among them is the statistical clock, which looks for technologically mediated catastrophes in real time on internet news sites (train accidents, gun crimes, plane crashes, etc.). When it finds a disaster, this black, blob-shaped device, made of acoustical foam, starts to count in a computerized voice, breaking the silence and reconnecting us with the real meaning of these abstract statistics. S.O.C.D. (Sexual Obsessive Compulsive Disorder) is an object for people who enjoy pornography but feel guilty about doing so. Presented as a sort of black, boxed DVD player, it also has a long, shiny, rubbery, dildo-pink shape protruding from it towards the viewer's chair. The object is meant to play pornographic

material and the appendage to sense and monitor the viewer's state of arousal. As the viewer becomes aroused, the video and sound increasingly pixelate, forcing the viewer to calm down. But then the pixels cheekily reveal more of the image, arousing the viewer again, who is caught in a game of concealing and revealing, which parallels his contradictory feelings. The Exploder Object creates, at random, an abnormal situation in your living room. This white, box-shaped object stands there, doing nothing for months, indicating its live status only by a little pressure gauge on its side. When the planets are in the appropriate configuration, the device will explode, inflating a giant pink balloon in seconds – an unpredictable act, which no one may witness. The aftermath forces us out of our ordinary condition: a giant, deflated, pink volume lies on the floor, to be cleared up only when the intrusion has been savoured to the full.

[opposite, from left to right]
Robot No. 1, No. 3, No. 2, No. 4

[above]
Robot No. 3

More and more of our data, even our most personal and secret information, will be stored on digital databases. How do we ensure that only we can access it? This robot is a sentinel; it uses retinal scanning technology to decide who accesses our data. In films iris scanning is always based on a quick glance. This robot demands that you stare into its eyes for a long time; it needs to be sure it is you.

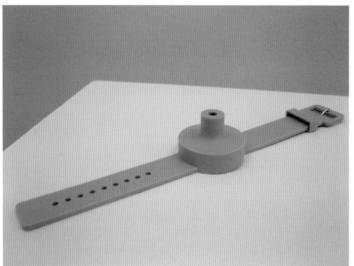

**Do You Want to Replace
the Existing 'Normal'?**
2007

In collaboration with
Michael Anastassiades

[above]
**S.O.C.D. (Sexual Obsessive
Compulsive Disorder)**

*Insert favourite porn DVD, hold sensor.
As excitement levels increase the image and
sounds becomes more pixelated*

[left]
Risk Watch

*When inserted into the ear, a small switch
is pressed and a voice reports the current
status. The 'Current Status' comes in different sizes, from the status of a country
under terrorist threat to a location status
of your lover or your child. The English
'BBC' voice softly in your ear provides the
necessary reassurance.*

Exploder Object

The days go by. The weeks go by. Months, even. Nothing. A small pressure gauge indicates it's operational. It could go off at any time. When the Planets are in the appropriate configuration, the airbag is filled, an explosion of pinkness. It takes seconds. Voluminous. Fantastic. A triclinic crystal. But no one sees it, only the aftermath. A landscape of shocking fluorescent pink rip-stock fabric, in sharp fractal forms, is strewn across the living room floor.

THE UNCLE PHONE

PRODUCTS INSPIRED
BY PECULIAR BEHAVIOURS

22 POP

EMAIL TYPEWRITER
FOR TECHNOPHOBES

APARNA RAO

Aparna Rao is a designer based in Bangalore, India. Mixing critical thinking, advanced technologies and art, her approach often stems from everyday observation but the devices come across as poetic, humorous and often slightly surreal, conveying a poignant vision of our technological world.

Her Uncle series is a set of six devices inspired by the peculiar habits of her real uncle, who, for instance, often asked Aparna to dial a phone number for him while he held the receiver expectantly. In response, Aparna designed this extra-long phone, which allows her to meet her uncle's demand remotely. Then, to assuage his fear of computers and technology, she wired up an old manual typewriter, an Olivetti Lettera 22, to make 22 Pop, the first typewriter that will also automatically send emails, making the task familiar and accessible.

These personal yet universal objects are imbued with love and care and represent a perhaps more feminine vision of technology, which may influence the way we consider and design electronic artefacts.

The Uncle Phone
2004

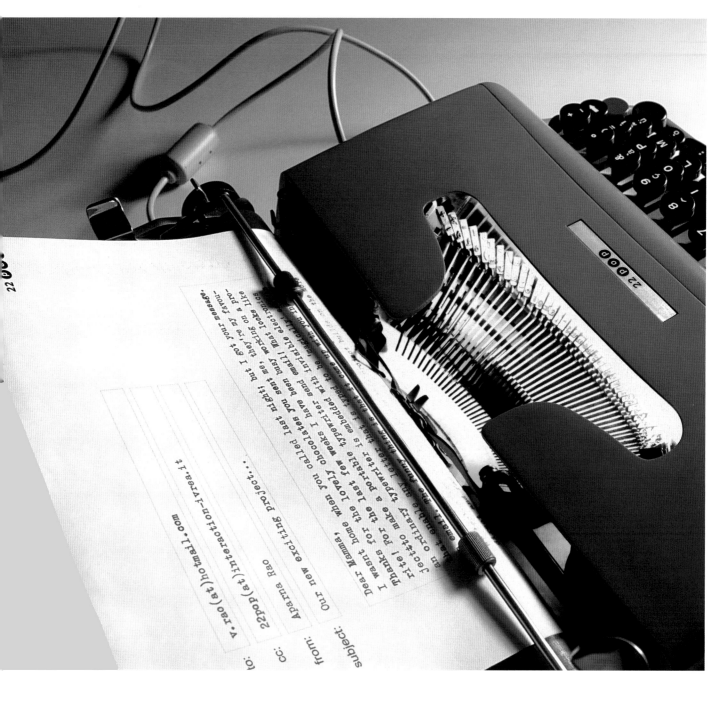

to: v.rao(at)hotmail.com

CC: 22pop(at)interaction-ivrea.it

from: Aparna Rao

subject: Our new exciting project...

Dear Mamma,

Thanks for the lovely chocolates I got your message. I wasn't home the last few weeks, when you called last night; but they're on a pro-
Thanks for the portable typewriter and sent busy. What electronic mess. How do I...

ZXZX
CHEATING PHYSICAL DEVICE
FOR COMPUTER GAMING

MR JONES
WATCHES
WATCHES WITH SOCIAL AND
PSYCHOLOGICAL FUNCTIONS

KATAZUKUE
SELF-CLEARING DESK
WITH CONVEYOR BELT

CRISPIN JONES

Crispin Jones is a fine example of a designer whose work allies critical thinking and products. With his iconic Mr Jones Watches, he explores the social and psychological functions of an object noted for its particularly rich cultural content, far exceeding its mere time-telling function. His first series of watches, intended as speculative objects, challenges the way we usually value our expensive time-pieces, which flatter our self-esteem and broadcast positive signals about our taste and affluence. The Summissus watch, for instance, alternately displays the time and the statement 'remember you will die', in an attempt to foster humility in the wearer. Adsiduus, pictured here, attempts to alter its wearer's personality by auto-suggestion. Another example, Fallax, is a watch with an integrated lie detector, which displays on its screen the wearer's honesty. Jones has created many other experimental watches and recently introduced a limited edition series of them.

His questioning of our behaviour towards electronics is a recurring theme in his work. ZXZX is a device designed to play the 1980s Olympics simulation 'track and field' game, which allows the player to achieve a world record in each of the events. Cheating is a central part of the virtual experience, especially in gaming (with codes and hardware autofire), but what does it mean to cheat the computer, an uncaring, blind opponent? How can this still engender feelings of elation at winning or frustration at losing? ZXZX encourages us to think about what it means to outwit the computer.

Another witty reflection on the non-rational, emotional relationships we have with our machines is Katazukue, the self-clearing table. Using a pair of powerful integrated conveyor belts, the table deposits everything put on it onto the floor. This is partly a commentary on the way tables are often, over the course of a day, set for different purposes and partly a comical metaphor of technology in general and the constant confrontation between the benefits it brings us and the things it damages or takes away.

Mr Jones Watches
2004

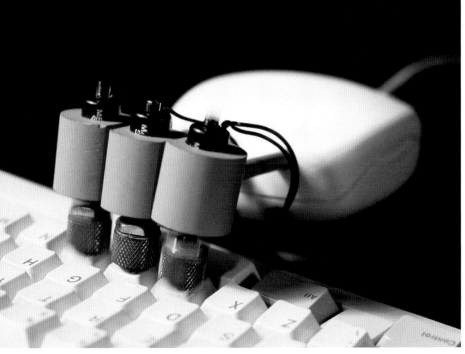

[above]
Katazukue
The tidy table
2005

[left]
ZXZX
1999

PEER PRESSURE
PROJECT   DEVICES TO DEFLECT
              PEER PRESSURE
ALICE WANG

With her Peer Pressure Project, designer Alice
Wang investigates how electronic devices could
help us to create a more charismatic public face,
thereby easing the pressure we feel to conform to
a norm instead of showing how we really are. The
double-sided headphone, for instance, enables us
to listen to very embarrassing music in public,
without having to worry if people around you can
hear it too. The headphone possesses two sets of
speakers, one playing your track inwards, the other
broadcasting some trendy music outwards to the
people around you. Popular Mobile is a subscription
service that will randomly send you messages to
make you look more popular in public. Fast-typing
Keyboard is a device for office cubicles that will
make your colleagues believe you are a real whiz-
kid, typing as fast as lightning. The last device in
this series is a printer-embedded software that
automatically filters your inbox and will send all
the emails that speak positively about you to the
office-shared printers. As your colleagues pick up
their prints, they will also accidentally see yours,
and that gets the gossip going. Can products prey
on our psychological weaknesses, and should they
be considered appropriate tools for our psychological
comfort? Peer Pressure Project is double-edged: on
the one hand the devices free us from perceived group
pressure while on the other they may reinforce the
notion of what is success and even raise the standard.

Peer Pressure Project
2007

[above]
Positive Printer

*This printer helps generate positive
rumours for you in the office. It filters
your email inbox and automatically
prints out all your positive emails. When
your colleagues pick up their print from
the shared printer, they accidentally see
your prints, which gets the gossip going.*

[opposite top]
Popular Mobile

*A phone that randomly receives text
messages to make you look popular
in public.*

Fast-typing Keyboard

*When you are in your office cubicle,
your colleagues often can't see you but
can vaguely hear you. This keyboard
is designed for those who are worried
about getting picked on about typing
too slowly.*

[opposite bottom]
Double-sided Headphones

*For when you want to listen to
embarrassing music but worried
people near you can hear it too. It plays
one track inwards and another track
outwards simultaneously.*

«…PEOPLE UNCONSCIOUSLY COMPARE THEIR OWN ATTITUDES, VALUES, INTERESTS AND PERSONALITY WITH OTHERS. CAN [THESE] PRODUCTS CREATE THE PERFECT PUBLIC PERSONALITY FOR US?» ALICE WANG

LOOKING FOR GOD FERNANDO ORELLANA

A SPIRITUAL ROBOT
LOOKING FOR GOD

Fernando Orellana's work often uses new media to deal with socio-political ideas, as in this installation, Looking for God. The origin of the idea of God has always been hotly debated by seekers of truth. While Creationists argue that the idea of God is inherent in us, Evolutionists believe that it was a way for primitive humankind to cope with a hostile and mysterious environment. Yet some would see an uncanny similarity between the search for God and the methodical scrutiny of our skies in search of alien signals. Although religions and philosophies differ in their attitudes, this seeking for truth is deeply ingrained in humans.

With Looking for God, Orellana ponders what this question might mean for an artificially made intelligence, should self-aware devices be one day possible. Would intelligent machines search for a deity, whether it be a god, aliens or another artificial intelligence? If so, how would they do it? Would they also inherit the desire to seek the truth from generation to generation? The installation consists of an old General Electrics radio, a microphone, an electronic odometer, an electronic bell, a microprocessor and a mechanism that is able to tune the radio. The mechanism turns the dial of the radio slightly, either to the left or right. The microphone then captures a three-second sample of the audio signal coming out of the radio. This captured signal is then compared to a signal saved in the microprocessor's memory of the word 'god'. If the new signal does not match the signal in memory, the mechanism turns the dial again and the process is repeated. If the signal captured does match, the piece deduces that it has found the word 'god'. It then triggers the electronic bell and marks one unit on the electronic odometer. In this way, Looking for God tries metaphorically to replicate humanity's own quest to understand the world.

Looking for God
2004

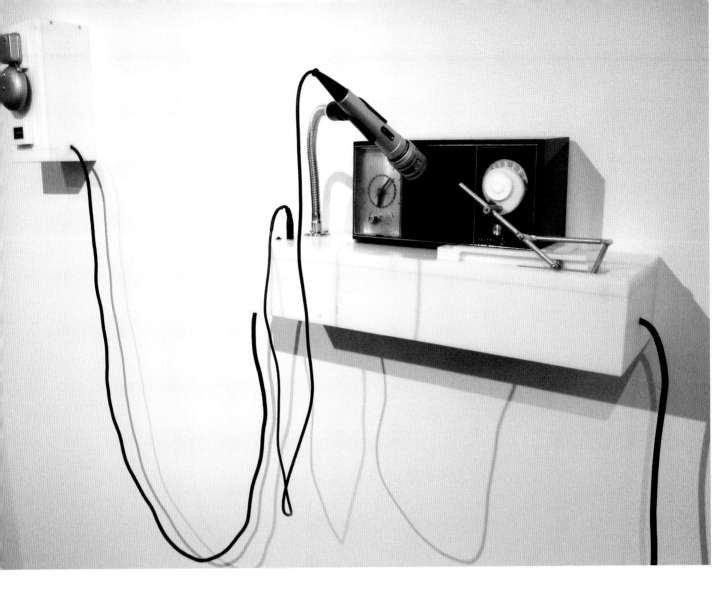

«I AM FASCINATED THAT THE HUMAN RACE IS LOOKING FOR ALIENS IN RADIATION, INCLUDING RADIO WAVES. I FOUND THAT THIS PURSUIT IS ANALOGOUS TO THE SEARCH FOR RELIGION OR GOD. I WONDERED, IF A SELF-AWARE ARTIFICIAL INTELLIGENCE WAS POSSIBLE, WOULD IT ALSO BECOME OBSESSED WITH THE 'GOD' IDEA?» FERNANDO ORELLANA

STEALTH
PRODUCTS
SOCIAL WEAPONS INSPIRED
BY MILITARY DESIGNS
CORPORATE
SABOTAGE
WEAPONS FOR THE
CORPORATE WORLD
KOK-CHIAN LEONG

With his projects Corporate Sabotage and Stealth
Products, Kok-Chian Leong suggests an alternative
context for weapon technologies that lies between
the military and the commercial market. Corporate
Sabotage is a series of weapons for the corporate
world, aimed at the competitive professional who
seeks promotion by inflicting a non-lethal trauma
on his co-workers, thereby enabling him to get
ahead in business. The project questions private
politics in the corporate world, an environment
where competitiveness can turn into deceit. It
focuses on the act of sabotaging office communications
and equipment by reducing their efficiency. Firefly
is a modified scanner incorporating an intermittently
flashing light that can be remotely activated to
produce imperfect scanned documents that have
white streaks running through the image.
Woodpecker, a modified printer, can similarly
sabotage documents by introducing print marks
and black patches on them, to the frustration of
its victims. To monitor these tricks, Kok-Chian has
developed a third tool, a wireless camera concealed
in a conventional-looking folder, which can be
placed nearby.

Stealth Products is a series of devices that employ
military design thinking in a socio-cultural context.
Shapeshifter, for example, is a psychological weapon
for women to protect them in potentially threatening
situations. It is capable of instantly inflating, like
an air bag, temporarily changing the shape of the
wearer's body to suggest that she is heavily pregnant,
thereby, it is hoped, invoking a cultural immunity
to acts of aggression. Another of the series is an
anti-photography spray, which uses ultra-reflective
nano-particles to scatter the light and thus obstruct
facial photography.

[opposite]
Stealth Products
Shapeshifter
2006

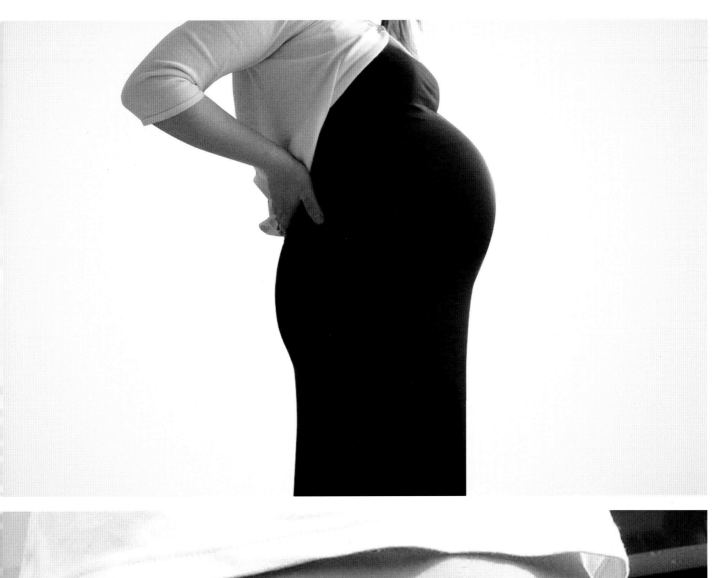

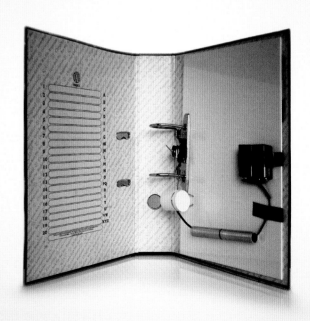

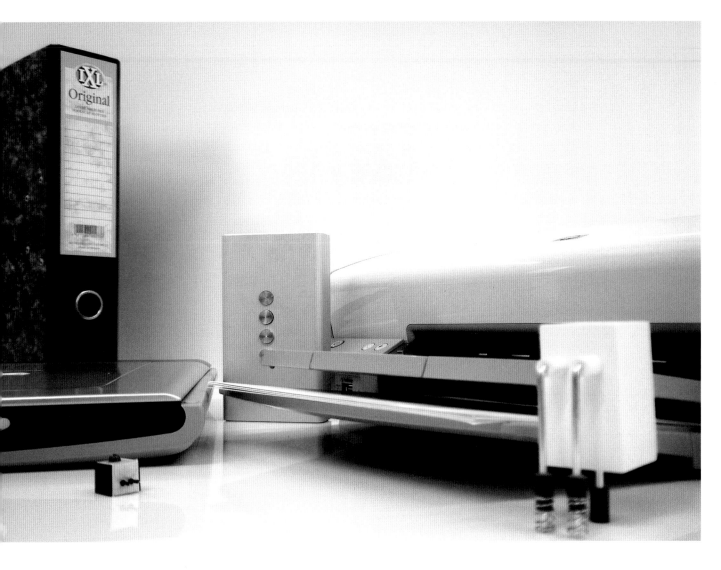

Corporate Sabotage
Weapons for the corporate armoury
2005

[opposite top]
Woodpecker

*This tool produces irregular stamping
action in the printer, which causes
patches in the final printout, rendering
it useless.*

[opposite bottom]
Cateye

*This tool is the eye of the saboteur.
It is a spy camera that provides a visual
overview of the victim's actions and
intentions. It has to be strategically
placed within the operations area.*

[above, from left to right]
**Cateye, Firefly, Remote Control,
Woodpecker**

PRECISION
TOASTER
TOASTER FOR THE
PERFECTION-OBSESSED
HARI &
PARKER
SPY TOYS OF THE FUTURE
ONKAR KULAR

As our technological objects become more and more intelligent, we see them starting to recognize us, through presets, custom functions and dedicated logins, and perhaps tomorrow through little RFID tags that we will carry around with us. These objects adjust themselves to our preferences, from custom desktop environments and telephone shortcuts to room temperature and so on. In his Machines for Living series, designer Onkar Singh Kular investigates the banal rituals of the everyday, aiming to challenge our perception of individual perfection, and the point at which mundane objects become less about psychological or physical comfort and more about obsession. Part of this series, Precision Toaster is a machine electronically enhanced with a preset function that allows every user in the household to store his/her exact preferred toasting time. The device is sold with a pack of sliced bread, for setting up experiments and defining the correct preset times. By verging on the grotesque, the machine successfully captures our attention and gets us thinking about our everyday habits

The same process is used in another piece, commissioned by the Science Museum in London for an exhibition entitled 'The Science of Spying'. As part of a campaign to get the audience thinking about the implications of surveillance and spying technologies, Onkar created Hari & Parker, two fictional toy characters who encourage children to commit subtle acts of domestic surveillance. The cute characters are sold with their own surveillance-themed children's books and fully functioning spy toy merchandise.

[above]
Precision Toaster
2002

[opposite]
Hari & Parker
2007

In collaboration with graphic designer
Anthony Burrill and artist Wilfrid Wood

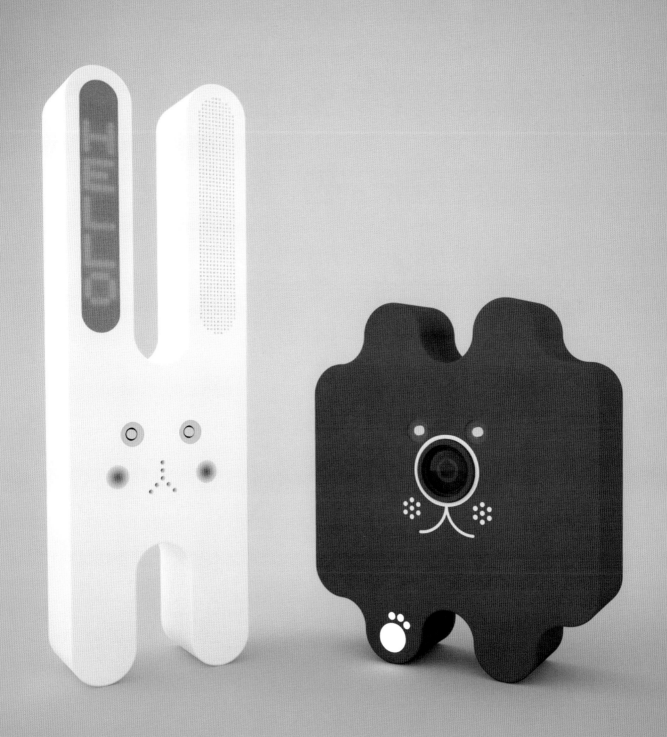

NAKI SERIES
ONTOLOGICAL DEVICES

TSUKUBA SERIES
WEIRD AND WONDERFUL
ELECTROMECHANICAL
MUSICAL INSTRUMENTS

EDELWEISS SERIES
DEVICES AS FICTIONAL PROPS

MAYWA DENKI

Maywa Denki is a Japanese art unit, which has created a series of unconventional and fascinating devices and toys that demonstrate an intricate social critique and often deal with psychological and ontological themes. Their collection of Naki devices, for instance, started as a reflection on the nature of the self. To try to answer the question 'Who am I?', Nobumichi Tosa – the actual 'president' of the unit – started with the dada-esque strategy of comparing himself to a fish. Each Naki created is one possible answer to the question, and by examining all the devices – 26 in total, alphabetically ordered – Tosa hoped to create a complete image of himself and a portrayal of the intricacies of his mind. The theme of the fish, if apparently quite arbitrary for a Western observer, has a particular resonance in Japanese culture. Furthermore, the exceptional craft and unique formal language with which the objects are realized, their humour, wit and underlying critique of Japanese society make them exceptional, multilayered, technological artefacts that are both amusing and thought-provoking. Seen here is Sei-Gyo (Naki-XX), a fish-controlled vehicle. The position of the fish inside the cross-shaped tank on the top is monitored by sensors, which in turn control the caterpillars' movement, jolting the vehicle around awkwardly. The device enables the fish to evolve in a hostile terrestrial environment, becoming both the representation of a state of mind and a critique about the very nature of our technological efforts. The apparent nonsensical element is also present in Tako-Niwa (Naki-RX), a kooky musical fish tank with rotating laser that triggers electrically controlled mallets placed in its periphery when a fish swimming inside the tank intercepts the laser beam. This particular Naki is also used to operate a typewriter, Koi-bumi (Naki-WX), which creates nonsense fish novels.

Naki Series

Naki-AX
Hammer-Head
1997

75 x 49 x 20 cm (29 x 19 x 8 in.)

Punch-card data is read to move the electromagnet that controls the movement of the carp in formalin.

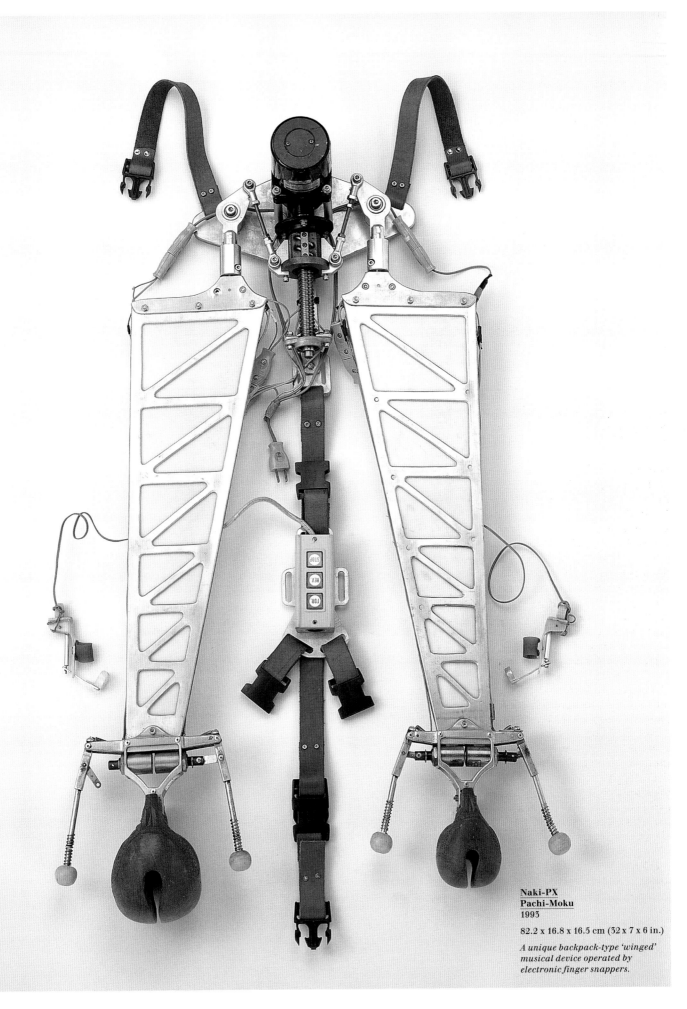

Naki-PX
Pachi-Moku
1993

82.2 x 16.8 x 16.5 cm (32 x 7 x 6 in.)

*A unique backpack-type 'winged'
musical device operated by
electronic finger snappers.*

Named in homage to the Japanese high-tech city,
the Tsukuba series consists of some two dozen
electromechanical musical devices, which are
computer-controlled through motors and
electromagnets. These highly original instruments,
which combine invention and craft, aim to reconcile
music with a material substance in an age where
music is increasingly digital and computer-generated.
Among the instruments, which Maywa Denki often
use in concerts, are the fantastic-looking Guitar-la,
in which six acoustic guitars are arranged in a fan-
like contraption and controlled by an organ,
Takedamaru, a saxophone-like instrument made
of old car horns, and Taratter, an enhanced pair
of tap shoes with additional 'knockers' controlled
by small keyboards strapped on to the wrist. The
Tsukuba series seems at times an extension of the
musical Nakis, which also include musical devices
such as Pachi-Mok and Koi-Beat, a carp-shaped
electromechanical beat-generator.

With the Edelweiss Series, Maywa Denki advances
its multilayered approach, albeit in a more allegorical
fashion. The devices are inspired by a philosophical
fairy tale written by Nobumichi, a twisted, Orwellian
tale of birth, rebellion and death, which presents a
symbolic vision of a technologically driven society
consumed by consumerism. The tale disturbingly
comments on our urge to create beautiful, albeit
environmentally harmful objects, despite the
existence of less aesthetically pleasing alternatives.
The objects in the Edelweiss Series are more or less
literally derived from the story, hence acting as props
existing in this fantastic world.

Maywa Denki's original approach extends to the way
they embrace the distribution of their work through
mass-production. The art unit is organized as a small
electrical company, and Nobumichi Tosa always
appears publicly in the traditional Japanese turquoise
electrical shop outfit. Their pieces are called 'products',
which they show during 'product demonstrations' –
exhibitions or live performances using their objects.
The process is an ingenious blend of art, marketing
and entertainment. The original artworks are
transformed into real products, toys, DVDs, CDs,
books, clothes…. The unit has inspired a whole
generation of Japanese artists and designers, now
grouped under the label of device art.

[above]
Naki-RX
Tako-Niwa
1995

120 x 210 x 120 cm (47 x 83 x 47 in.)

*Light-activated rhythm knocker operated
by the movement of a fish. The knocker
works when the fish accidentally
intercepts a laser spinning in the top
of the aquarium.*

[opposite top]
MI-03
Taratter
1993

17 x 39 x 10 cm (7 x 15 x 4 in.)

*Remote-controlled tap shoes that enable
anybody to tap very easily. The tapping
sound is made by controlling the
knocker set on the toe with your fingers.*

[opposite bottom]
Naki-XX
Sei-Gyo (Holy Fish)
1994

17.5 x 41 x 31 cm (7 x 16 x 12 in.)

*Fish-controlled tractor vehicle in the
shape of a cross. The caterpillar moves
in the same direction as the fish swims.*

[above]
Seamoons
Anna, Betty and Clara
2004

75 x 18.5 x 75 cm (29 x 7 x 29 in.)

Singing machine. The bellows sends air into an artificial vocal cord made of rubber, in which tension is controlled by a computer program.

[opposite]
Marimca
2001

73 x 82 x 26.2 cm (29 x 32 x 10 in.)

An 'open-and-close' self-striking marimba. When playing, the flowers open; when finished, the flowers close.

ELECTROPROBE
A GATEWAY TO THE
ELECTROMAGNETIC
WORLD

TROIKA

The Electroprobe allows its user to access the immaterial world of data by picking up the electromagnetic radiations generated by electronic devices and amplifying them directly into sound. Each time an electric current is established or cut in a circuit, tiny electromagnetic waves are emitted. This phenomenon is partly responsible for the electro-smog that surrounds us and our electronic objects. As devices become more sophisticated, their inaudible language, magnetic hums and electric whispers, become larger and more varied. By revealing a soundscape never heard before, the Electroprobe urges its user to revaluate her electronic surroundings. It creates contradictory feelings, between a fascination with the discovery of this parallel sonic world and the disturbing realization of being continuously immersed in large and possibly dangerous magnetic fields.

To intensify these feelings still further, a special playground called Shit! I Forgot the iPod! was created for the Electroprobes: a gallery installation where all available electronic and electrical objects typical of a small flat were placed and re-arranged. Due to the number of objects, the electric power consumed was 6,000 W, thereby creating a huge magnetic field. The devices were arranged according to their magnetic noises to produce a rich, varied soundscape to be explored and performed with the Electroprobes. The fridge created bass, warm sounds at intervals, the computer scanner generated high-pitched whistlings and the fans started to interfere with the nearby TV to create loud, percussive rhythms. Electromagnetic melodies were performed by a drill, a neon light and a heater – all building to an apparently chaotic assemblage and thoroughly intriguing soundscape.

5/INTERVIEWS

Fictional functions and functional fictions
Dunne & Raby

Bringing ice to Macondo
Ron Arad

Technology as a raw material
Steven Sacks

Device art – media art meets mass production
Machiko Kusahara

FICTIONAL FUNCTIONS AND FUNCTIONAL FICTIONS
DUNNE & RABY

Authors of the seminal book Design Noir: The secret life of electronic objects, designers Anthony Dunne and Fiona Raby use products and services as a medium to stimulate discussions among designers, industry and the public about the social, cultural and ethical implications of emerging technologies. They experiment by designing for the complex nature of human beings, with all their irrational and often contradictory emotions, in an attempt to draw attention to issues that mass production typically ignores.

Troika: Do you think that artists and designers in this book are pioneering a new approach to how technology is thought about, its function and its role in our society?

D&R: At the time of writing, a design trend is emerging: design exhibitions of big shapes, expensive shapes, impressive shapes. Some people like them, some people don't. Sometimes they look like chairs or tables, but not always. They are extensions of designers' egos. Often labelled 'design art', they are art without the art. It feels like the end of something, the slow-motion implosion of a formalist approach that has dominated furniture design for the last part of the 20th century.

These mute, autistic objects radiate ignorance of the world around us. They're apolitical and content free. But design/art doesn't have to be like this.

This book contains designs for the 21st century: embryonic, complex, challenging, fresh. They move beyond obsessions with shape, form and material to embrace behaviour, interactivity and our internal worlds on individual and mass scales. They are both art and design and full of content.

Products are the currency of today's consumer society; they surround us, shaping and mediating our experiences, dreams, fantasies and desires. Five to ten years ago many of the product ideas expressed in this book would have been fake products connected by cables to boxes of electronics sitting behind a nearby wall. Making installations was the main option open to artists and designers exploring technology's functional and aesthetic potential. Now, at last, designers and artists can prototype actual products even if only as one-offs, narrowing the gap between experimental design thinking and everyday life. This has become possible due to recent technological developments that make prototyping more accessible and affordable – the availability of new prototyping systems like Arduino, coding languages like processing, advances in wirelessness, 3D rapid prototyping and the possibility of fabricating low-cost PCBs in China.

But the most important thing about the projects in this book is that they are
fully engaged with the world around us – socially, politically, culturally and
technologically. They are deeply human, challenging, meaningful and reflective.
They are issue-based rather than purely formalistic. And they offer a refreshing
alternative to narrow corporate visions of the role technology could play in our lives.

Troika: It seems to us that most of the designers and artists in this book follow
an experimental, subjective design process. How does this translate to the end
result?

D&R: Each project is a testament to the impossibility of the possible. They offer up
richer experiences and embody values far broader than those available in existing
mass-market products. Yet although nearly all the items in this book could be
mass-manufactured, they are unlikely to be. They remind us that the reason many
experimental designs are not taken up for mass production is less to do with technical
and economic feasibility and more to do with difficult content that challenges the
status quo.

Troika: Do you think they participate in creating richer, more complex products?

D&R: Absolutely.

Troika: What do you believe is their relevance?

D&R: They provide a space where new ideas about how we interact with each other,
technology and culture can be tested, presented and communicated – a parallel design
channel or genre dedicated to ideas. In them, we catch glimpses of how things could
be if industry was a bit more imaginative and in tune with how people actually are.

Troika: Designer as author: how does it work?

D&R: Every product is authored. Without design authorship, product development is
driven purely by economic and market forces. By assuming authorship designers can
subvert this process. Subjectivity is commonly understood as a bad thing in design,
understandably so when it so often results in mere self-expression and egomania. But
being an author is not about ego; that's an old-fashioned view of authorship, it's about
a designer being involved in the definition of values that are embedded in an object.
Questioning the implications of ideas and ideologies locked into the operation of a
product. With electronics we are not simply talking about form and visual aesthetics,
but the function of the product, and what it allows us to do and what it prevents us
from doing.

Just like literature, authoring does not have to mean the reader assumes a passive
and uncreative role. As many of the projects in this book demonstrate, there are lots
of ways of designing that allow for interpretation and creative misuse: abuser-
friendliness rather than user-friendliness.

Troika: What is the benefit of it?

D&R: Humanization. Authoring ensures human content. The designer as author is an
advocate for all that is human, messy, contradictory and irrational. Without it we get
pure technology, marketing and economics.

Troika: What is critical design?

D&R: Critical design uses speculative design proposals to challenge narrow
assumptions, preconceptions and givens about the role products play in everyday
life. It is more of an attitude than anything else, a position rather than a method.
There are many people doing this who have never heard of the term 'critical design'
and who have their own way of describing what they do. Naming it 'critical design'
is simply a useful way of making this activity more visible and subject to discussion
and debate. Its opposite is 'affirmative design': design that reinforces the status quo.
Design as critique has existed before under several guises. Italian radical design

of the 1970s for instance, was highly critical of prevailing social values and design ideologies. Critical design builds on this attitude and extends it into today's world. Some relatives are: activism, cautionary tales, conceptual design, contestable futures, design fictions, interrogative design, radical design, satire, social fiction, speculative design.

Troika: What questions does it raise?

D&R: It's not just about asking questions. Its main purpose is to make us think. But also to raise awareness, expose assumptions, provoke action, spark debate and even entertain in an intellectual sort of way, like literature or film.

Troika: Why today?

D&R: The world we live in today is incredibly complex. Our social relations, desires, fantasies, hopes and fears are very different from those at the beginning of the 20th century. The role technology plays today in shaping our experience of everyday life is unprecedented. Yet many key ideas underpinning contemporary design practice stem from the early 20th century.

Troika: Why is critical design interested in technology?

D&R: Society has moved on but design has not. Critical design is one of many mutations design is undergoing in an effort to remain relevant to the complex technological, political, economic and social changes we are experiencing now. Rather than speeding up the entry of technology into everyday life, we need to reflect on its impact and ask if we even need it. Critical design is one way of doing this.

Troika: Is critical design only an academic exercise or do you think its outcomes could/should enter the mass market? Is this important at all?

D&R: Although fundamentally academic, there's no reason its outcomes cannot be mass-produced. It is not anti-industry nor anti-mass production; it's a strategy that places emphasis on combining content and aesthetics. It can be issue-based, awareness-raising or thought-provoking. These can be a product's sole function or they can be combined with other levels of use, purpose and meaning.

Troika: Do you think designers have to develop fully functioning prototypes or be limited by available technology?

D&R: Dogma is the problem, not prototyping.

If you are designing for now, for today, then it is essential you build your idea and test it. If you are designing for the future, prototyping the future, if you like, then probably not, at least not in the way we think of usually: we can simulate and fake experiences instead. It's important to ask what needs to be tested and why, and then think of the best way of achieving it. This could be by making a fully working technical prototype, but not always. Scenarios are prototypes too, for testing a vision. So are videos.

'Demo or die' is a dogma. The belief that technical prototyping is the only way of developing an idea quickly becomes a problem when it prevents designers from engaging with technologies beyond their level of ability, budget or means. The result of this dogma for people without the luxury of a lab will always be small, craft-like objects: a form of digital craft. There's nothing wrong with this, but sometimes we need to turn our attention to problems and ideas that are bigger and more complex than we can handle individually or make ourselves. These skills are important too.

Designers shouldn't let the fact we can't build working prototypes prevent us from engaging with emerging technologies like bio- and nanotech. Just because we can't get our hands on them (yet) doesn't mean we shouldn't get involved with them.

Troika: Why do you think technology companies do not produce designer items or hire individual designers as much as furniture companies do?

D&R: Although there seemed to be a moment in the 1960s when electronic products – radios and TVs mainly – were embraced by the furniture world and briefly became vehicles for aesthetic experimentation, today, electronics are not really viewed as cultural artefacts in the way that, for instance, furniture and clothing are, but as disposable objects doomed to rapid obsolescence. This book is full of examples that show this does not have to be the case.

Troika: In a world saturated by functional objects and gadgets pretending functionality, do you think that creating objects that look to more psychological needs, whether they are intricate ones or mere entertainment, is the only way forward to sustain production and ensure market leadership?

D&R: Focusing on new or neglected psychological needs is definitely one way forward. Gadgets already do this and that's why they are so amusing and interesting. A look through any gadget catalogue affords a fascinating portrait of modern life and what it means to be human today. All our fears, anxieties and obsessions are manifest in wonderfully strange products. Now if only they were beautifully designed!

We're very interested in the difference between fictional functions and functional fictions. The former is what we get every day – functional products that meet fictional needs. The mobile phone is a perfect example: we don't need half the functions it offers us. They are pure fictions created to sell more bandwidth. On the other hand, many of the projects in this book we would describe as functional fictions. They do not exist as 'real' products, but as prototypes, semi-real, fictional, but these fictions are highly functional and the needs they meet, although often intellectual, are real and genuine.

Troika: What challenges do you think face this type of art and design in the near future?

D&R: To not get stuck in a 'digital art/design' ghetto, which could easily happen if designers and artists continue to define their identity in relation to particular technologies – new media design, digital design, computer art, bio art, nano art, interactive art. Designers working in this area have excellent experience of dealing with the trickiness of design for new technology and making it relevant and meaningful to people's daily lives. We need to continue to embrace new technologies, apply our learning to them and learn to feel comfortable moving across different technological platforms. The end of the 20th century was a small-scale rehearsal for more complex challenges facing us in the 21st century. The designers and artists in this book are perfectly positioned to help achieve technological futures that reflect the complex, troubled people we are, rather than the easily satisfied consumers and users we are supposed to be.

BRINGING ICE
TO MACONDO
RON ARAD

One of the most influential designers of our time, Ron Arad has consistently avoided categorization by curators and critics throughout his career. Whether as architect, furniture or product designer, he is continually innovative and challenging, combining form with advanced technologies.

Alongside his limited-edition studio work, Ron Arad designs for many leading international companies such as Vitra, Moroso, Alessi and Cappellini. Some of his latest architectural projects include the National Design Musuem, currently on site in Holon, Israel; Y's (Yohji Yamamoto) flagship store, Tokyo; the Maserati Ferrari headquarters showroom in Modena; the living room and family dining room for Sheikh Saud Al-Thani of Qatar; and the Selfridges Technology Hall, London.

Troika: What do you think about the approach/process the designers and artists in this book have developed? Designers and artists have always been using technology, especially technologies of production, but this seems to be the first time that digital, electronic and more generally information technology is being so widely employed in material artefacts. Do you see a shift in the approach there?

RA: We live in a time where everything is digital. Digital technology is commonplace. When I grew up we had one telephone in the neighbourhood, and then there was a public one in the pharmacy. The next generation was born with the telephone and television in their home. Now, every time you read an interview with a celebrated photographer, the inevitable question is: are you going digital or not? We drive cars, we don't use horses. Technology is everywhere. There was a time when you tried to see what you could do with technology. This was very exciting. Now we have the benefit of being blasé about it. We can start to look into what it is about and why it is interesting. You go to a rock concert and have digital screens everywhere. We are going to be more demanding, because we are spoiled with choices. It is like bringing ice to Macondo in One Hundred Years of Solitude. Thinking of my personal work, when you could do things like this for the first time, it was exciting. It was exciting to discover a new process or material, but it's all part of what you do. The worst thing that could have happened to me and to us would have been if we had got hooked on it. You can get hooked on a tool and the effect.

Troika: Digital is nothing new and it's true that it is pervasive. You are saying that it is unavoidable that designers would enter that territory, and it feels as if now, for the first time, there is a real reflection on what the technology brings, its use and impacts, beyond the realm of possibilities and the 'wow' effect.

RA: Everything in this book is fascinating and interesting. But I remember when synthesizers where new: it made everyone a musician. I think a lot of digital manufacturing made a lot of people create all sorts of fruits of the software. You look at lots of stuff that is being produced now. There is this wonderful word 'design art'. It's mindless. We know we can make a blob. We can all take a lump of marble and CNC-machine it to make it organic. It puts lots of people in a good mood; it puts me in a bad mood.

Troika: So what fascinates you in digital technologies? How and why do you use
them? Where do you see their relevance?

RA: [Referring to his new exhibition designs] It is pretty amazing that everything was
originated here, on this desk, not only the pieces, but also the graphics, the light. We
have seen everything here before. We have seen the digital version of it and then the
actual piece. Yes, there is a lot of digital processing in the process, but it is still
followed by an incredible amount of manual work. It is easy to get something to look
super-reflective on the computer. To get it super-reflective in the end, somebody still
has to polish it.

Troika: So for you, it is pretty much a tool. Your earlier work, at the time of
'One-off', for instance, involved a lot of direct manual work on the pieces, and,
as with any physical process, there are inherent trials and errors, mistakes and
discoveries, surprises that happen along the way and enrich and inform the design
process. A lot of people in the book apply this very approach towards digital
technology. On the other hand, the process you are describing is planned, in such
a way that you know exactly what the piece is going to look like. How do you feel
about this?

RA: [Digital technologies] give you a lot more possibilities. For me personally, the tool
is still very much the pencil, even though I mostly draw with a light pen rather than
with a 6B pencil, but the process is still very similar, only the tools are more
sophisticated. The paper is better, the pen is better, the palette is sort of richer. In
a funny way, the more sophisticated the machine gets, the less machine-like the
product becomes. In the old days when you did a drawing on the computer it would
look like a computer drawing but now I can do a drawing and experts will swear it
is a watercolour. And next year it will be even easier, because some people in Silicon
Valley will work on it. We always said that to make something you need to have an
idea first of something you want to do and then look for a way to do it: materials,
processes, engineers, technicians, wizards, people who can help you do it. The other
way is that of the wizard: the technologies come to you and you think about what can
be done with them. Two different ways, which are to me still very similar. I had an
idea of doing something, a piece based on an old-fashioned idea of negative and
positive. I wanted components that were a positive and a negative of each other and
yet, functionally, were exactly the same. On the computer it is dead easy to achieve
this, and easy to produce, but then you are looking for a clever way of doing it, not just
a possible way of doing it. It has to be a process that satisfies me.

Troika: Still, it feels very different from hammering a piece of metal and seeing
it behaving in a way you haven't foreseen. How does the material and tools process
compare to the digital one you are describing?

RA: There are a lot of surprises, a lot of happy accidents on-screen too. There is more
time on-screen. It's like working on a canvas that is always wet. Nothing is final. You
can decide on-screen what colour to apply, whereas when you do it with the real thing
it's done, final. So it is like tinkering with the real thing but it is more open-ended.
Let's stretch it this way or that way. You can't do this with a piece of metal. Can we try
to make it like this or like that? Now, we are designing an exhibition at the Pompidou
Centre, and approaching the space on the computer is like approaching a canvas. It
makes things a lot easier on the production side too. Before, I would have needed the
artisan. There are no artisans any more to improve or to make it work. We are losing
the artisan. And that's a shame because they introduced a lot of their vision too. There
was a time in Italy when you could recognize the artisan before you would recognize
the designer, like the legendary Sacchi, the model maker who did anything from the
Vespa to [furniture pieces for] Albini. They deserve a lot of respect. But now I am
pretty happy that we don't depend on them so much any more. And I feel bad when I go
to Italy and work on a product and I see someone making a model in wood and I say,
'Look, CNC it'. I am not sure if I am doing the right thing.

Not Made by Hand Not Made in China
2000
Produced by The Gallery Mourmans

All the objects you see in this collection were 'grown' in a tank by computer-controlled laser beams.

Lolita
for Swarovski Crystal Palace Collection, Milan, Italy, 2004

Drawing

2,100 crystals, 1,050 white LEDs embedded in the crystal, 1 km of nine-ways cable braided shielding and 31 processors
154.4 x 94.5 x 85.8 cm
(61 x 37 x 34 in.)

Troika: Some people in the book are also creating custom tools, like Front [p. 48] and Golembewski [p. 170]. The outcome could have not been done on screen or in Photoshop. Many people in the book are designing not only the outcome but also the hardware: they are creating tools. It breaks from a tradition of mere packaging design for electronics. Don't you think it has its own relevance when it comes together with concept and quality?

RA: It's nice to know that there is no other piece or technique that can do this, but that doesn't make or break the piece. I would be very bored if there was nothing more there than the technology.

Troika: Besides using the technology as a tool, you also seem to be incorporating it in the final pieces. Can you tell us more about Lolita [p. 31] and Lo-Rez-Dolores [pp. 32–35]? What was the starting point? What were your motivations?

RA: Lolita was very exciting in the beginning and also triggered people's imagination, but there was nothing magic there, nothing unusual, technologically speaking. When I was approached by Swarovski I told them that I had no connection with their product, that I am not interested in crystals, that I spend a lot of time avoiding their vitrines in Vienna airport. And then the next year came and I said OK and thought that, to make it appealing to me, I had to connect it to the things I was interested in at that time. At the time I was working on Lo-Rez-Dolores. In a way, Lolita is more interesting to me than Lo-Rez-Dolores, because it is not only about the technology, it has something else, because people for some reason enjoy interacting with the piece. It makes you think that it goes to a satellite. But it can't be exciting any more, the technology bit is not exciting any more. Another example is rapid-prototyping. At the end of the 1990s, we started playing with rapid-prototyping and animations of vases in [Autodesk®] Maya, where every frame can give you a new thing or you can create text through elimination. The process and the discovery were exciting at the time. Hopefully some of the fruits of that excitement remain for a while and then it becomes commonplace and not interesting any more. This is like my animated floor for the sheikh: there were a few things that led to it, an interest in low resolution.

Troika: Alongside these more experimental, one-off pieces, your work also comprises mass-manufactured products. A lot of your designs enter the commercial realm, but it's not quite the same with your digital pieces. I know you tried, quite a long time ago, to design a sort of versatile tablet PC. What was your experience of that?

RA: With the tablet PC we were a bit unlucky, and unprofessional with it too. But if you look now at the [Apple] iPod touch, it is a small version of it.

Troika: Electronic technologies are increasingly mediating our lives. However, although furniture companies are traditionally approaching designers to create products for them, you rarely see electronics companies approaching designers other than in-house design teams. Why do you think this is? Do you think this will evolve?

RA: It's because the design of electronic products is not just about the author; it's about the market, the user, the people. We as scholars now know all these things around us. I don't think the users really care about this.

TECHNOLOGY AS A RAW MATERIAL
STEVEN SACKS

Steven Sacks is the founder of the very first gallery ever devoted to what has been variously termed new media art, digital art, interactive art and software art. bitforms gallery opened in 2001, becoming the first fine art gallery devoted to new media art practices. Breaking new ground, the gallery became the destination for artists, curators and collectors exploring new art forms that lie at the intersection of innovative processes and mixed media. The gallery has become internationally recognized for its focus and influence on fresh territories of contemporary art practice.

Troika: What brought you to open bitforms, and why?

SS: I am the third generation of art dealers in my family. The previous generations had a very different sense of what art is. They were antique dealers. Everything was very precious, using traditional ideas, forms and media. Of course nothing in the house could be touched or interacted with. I learned to appreciate quality, craft and the business of art and that I also wanted to do something a little different.

In 1995 I co-founded Digital Agency Digital Pulp, in which, as a creative director, I managed the merger of the world of the programmers and that of the fine artists. This combination of traditional art processes and new media is what inspired me to open bitforms gallery. My instincts were supported by a number of high-profile new media museum shows that occurred in 2000–1. I felt something needed to be done to educate the curator and collector in the commercial art realm. After researching the galleries in NY, I felt I could offer a unique space with a clear focus on new media.

Troika: How can using digital tools or new media enhance the artistic process?

SS: Digital tools are sometimes utilized but do not define the work. This can be seen through advanced technologies or issues that are affecting and changing the way we live. It is important for the artists to push the definition of the media they are working in. This philosophy can be manifested through a photograph, drawing or huge interactive installation.

The use of software in an artist's practice is probably the most influential advancement in contemporary art. There are two elements of software worth differentiating. One is the improvement of off-the-shelf software to help artists with the creative process within the realms of photography, sculpture, collage, etc. These tools have helped to re-define and streamline the way many traditional artists work. The bigger leap forward is the use of custom software created by the artist as a tool, and it is typically derived from computer code written by the artist. The code is a set of rules or parameters; these rules can form the artwork and can be the essence of the experience and aesthetic direction. In traditional terms, the code represents paint or clay that the artist uses to create and similarly it is moulded, tweaked, massaged, layered until the artist is happy with the results. The results can vary drastically. The works can be simple. Complex. Abstract. Figurative. Narrative. Software can also take on many physical forms. It is important that the concept of the artwork still needs to be in the forefront of these new practices, although process can sometimes define the artistic intention.

Troika: How does the use of software affect the relationship between the art piece and its owner in comparison to more traditional tools?

SS: One of the most important distinctions is that software art is alive, which means the art is in essence alive. It is not a video loop or static experience. It can be interactive, reactive or passive. It is typically generative, which means it can build upon itself or through your interaction. Living with these works, especially interactive pieces, can seriously impact the daily life of the collector. Surveillance works by Lozano-Hemmer [p. 90], reflective mirror sculptures by Daniel Rozin [p. 83], sound sculptures by Peter Vogel [p. 126] all embody their spaces with personality and presence.

Troika: Do you think the appeal of the new media is based on novelty effect? How do you think this will evolve in time?

SS: I feel that new media are related to the time the artist creates the work and what is considered 'new' at that time. Artists have been exploring new processes in art for many decades. Many artists are 'one-hit wonders' who come up with a clever interaction or gadget. These artists do not have longevity in the fine art world. New media is a state of mind, a way of practising art. If the artist hones that practice over many years, alters ideas, forms and process, he or she will have a long career as an artist. When Daniel Rozin created his first mirror sculpture, many thought that was it, what else could he do? For the past ten years he has continued to make interactive mirror sculptures, each generation of work becoming more refined. The rigour and

Daniel Rozin
Shiny Balls Mirror
2003

Aluminium tubes, chrome-plated balls,
servo motors, video camera, computer
142 x 124 x 41 cm (56 x 49 x 16 in.)

exploration within each artist's practice will differ, but they all must have a focus
and discipline to erase the 'novelty effect'.

Troika: After a phase of purely screen-based digital art, we saw emerging artists
like Rozin, who explored analogue, physical devices as digital outputs. Do you see
there a paradigm shift in the artistic approach to technology?

SS: The exploration of the physical in new media is not really new. It's been part of the
art world for decades. It is true that access and efficiencies of new tools have allowed
certain artists to more easily focus on the integration of the physical form and new
media. But this focus on the physical is connected to each artist's practice and skill
set, and of course if the idea is better manifested with a solid form. I do believe that
new generations of artists will be offered different methods and tools early in their
careers, so that we will see a lot more variety in the mergers of media and sculpture.

Troika: As for you, how do the works of the artists you represent contribute to
expanding our understanding of technology and what it can be/do?

SS: Some are contributing a lens – a focused view of how their ideas are influenced
by technology's existence and how it's affecting the world we live in.

Troika: How do you choose the artists you represent?

SS: We represent both emerging and historically significant new media artists,
and emphasize diversity of media choice. How can photography, illustration, video,
sculpture evolve? We home in on artists who are pushing their chosen media to
new levels – re-inventing the past or defining new directions. bitforms gallery will
continue to search out artists who are exploring the most relevant contemporary
issues and employing new processes to achieve their creative vision. The accessibility
of technology and the global network of media and information will allow artists
to further investigate and create the next generation of 'new media' art.

DEVICE ART – MEDIA ART MEETS MASS PRODUCTION

MACHIKO KUSAHARA

Machiko Kusahara is a media art curator and a researcher in the field of media studies, who has been publishing and curating in the interdisciplinary field that embraces art, technology and culture. Her recent research focuses on the correlation between digital media and traditional culture. She coined the term 'device art' to describe an emerging movement of Japanese artists, many of whom feature in this book, who explore mass production and commercial circuits as a means of distribution of message-driven, individually-conceived technological artefacts.

Troika: What is device art, what does it aim at and what questions does it raise?

MK: Device art is a concept derived from the recent digital media art scene in Japan. Using both latest and everyday technologies and material, these media artworks enable users/viewers/interactors to enjoy and understand what media technologies mean to us. In device art, an artwork is realized in a form of device, the device becoming the content itself. Device art is a concept for re-examining art–science–technology relationships, from both a contemporary and a historical perspective, in order to foreground a new aspect of media art. The concept is a logical extension of a change in the notion of art that already started in the early 20th century with art movements such as Dada and Surrealism.

More recently, interactive art has redefined forms of art and the role of artists. What we call device art is a form of media art that integrates art and technology as well as design, entertainment and popular culture. There is a sense of playfulness or wonder in device artwork – even if it involves a serious theme – that makes it possible to be shown or commercialized outside museums and galleries. The concept reflects Japanese cultural tradition in many ways, including appreciation of refined tools and materials, love of technology, acceptance of playfulness and the absence of a clear border between art, design and entertainment, among other issues. Device art seeks after a new paradigm in art, by producing artworks based on creative use of hardware technologies and opening a channel to make them more accessible to everyone. Through these activities device art questions the validity of traditional boundaries between art, design, entertainment, technology and commercial products.

Troika: It seems that device art is about mass production of artworks. How does it differ, as a theory, from pop art?

MK: As described above, it is not just about mass production of artworks. Pop art responded to the mass-production/mass-consumption society. Its heritage can be seen in device art, with the use of industrial materials and media technologies, connection to pop culture, etc. But digital technology has changed our society further – and it still continues at an enormous speed. The impact is essential, with the very nature of 'being digital'. This is something different from the change in the society pop art dealt with. Needless to say, the idea of a 'virtual world' is commonplace now, what with avatars and other immaterial substitutes for the real world. Copies are not only massive but also identical; there is no distinction between original and copy, which means the traditional basis of 'art' has been challenged with digital technologies. Information became more important than physical materiality.

Device artists are responding to these issues. With their professional knowledge and skills in fields such as virtual reality, mechatronics, human interface and interactive technologies, they understand the possibilities and problems media technologies bring to us. It is also a reason why device art focuses on hardware-based work. Producing or delivering artwork widely is easier and more commonplace in software-based forms such as web art or games. The challenge for device art is to open such channels for physical objects.

Troika: As for you, how do the works of device artists expand our understanding of technology and what it can be/do? How can art devices contribute to how technology is thought about, its function and its role in our society?

MK: Artists visualize personal and social issues by providing different view angles from what we usually achieve in our daily life. Works of device artists expand our understanding of technology by realizing usually impossible experiences using their expertise. For example, Iwata's Floating Eye, literally realizes the McLuhanian 'extension of body' experience by combining latest technologies with old ideas such as walking with an eye mask. Works by Sachiko Kodama [pp. 124–27] or Masahiko Inami [1] transform known industrial materials into magical experiences. In all these examples, playfulness plays an important role. Japanese media artists have been often criticized for 'not being critical of technology'. But being critical does not necessarily mean being negative. Artists cannot stop technology by saying 'no'. Understanding technology is more important than denying. Generally speaking, media artists use media technology because they see many possibilities in it, as well as problems. It is possible for artists to show what technology can bring us, how interesting or amazing it can be when used creatively, how technology changes our life and society with possible problems. It is important that people become interested in technology and try to understand it, rather than being scared and using it only in a passive mode – or, even worse, being used by it. Artists can provide them with a key to understanding technology.

On the other hand, artists use and invent technology in ways engineers don't think about. Kodama's use of electromagnetic fluid is an example. We know many such cases in media art. Device art enhances such practice and helps to forge creative bonds between art, technology and science.

Troika: Considering the difficulties, both financial and technical, of getting an idea mass-produced, how much do you think an artwork has to be watered down for that purpose?

MK: It is a time- and effort-consuming process for an artist to make his or her artwork mass-produced. It also costs, to make prototypes, for example. Who will pay for these costs is always an issue. Private firms would not collaborate with an artist unless they saw a merit in it. To make anything widely distributed there are many factors to be considered and re-designed, including safety, durability, maintenance, etc. Although the cost of mass production should be covered within a normal business framework, public support for artists will help them to take the necessary time and effort to realize commercially acceptable products. At the same time, public support – both financial and schematic – is needed to facilitate joint projects between artists and engineers/scientists. Artists such as Nobumichi Tosa [p. 256], Kazuhiko Hachiya [2], Ryota Kuwakubo [p. 212] and Toshio Iwai [3] have realized their projects, but it's not always possible.

[1]
Professor Masahiko Inami is a Professor in the Department of Engineering and Intelligent Systems of the University of Electro-Communications, Tokyo. Together with Susumu Tachi and Naoki Kawakami he created a prototypical camouflage system, in which a video camera takes a shot of the background and displays it on a cloth using an external projector. The same year Time magazine named it the coolest invention of 2003.

[2]
Kazuhiko Hachiya is known for his art and technology experiments and inventions, from jet-powered hoverboards to abstract CG production.

[3]
Toshio Iwai is a Japanese interactive media and installation artist who has also created a number of commercial video games. He received high acclaim from critics for many of his musical performances and digital musical instrument designs, including the Tenori-On, a handheld device that plays sound and light patterns.

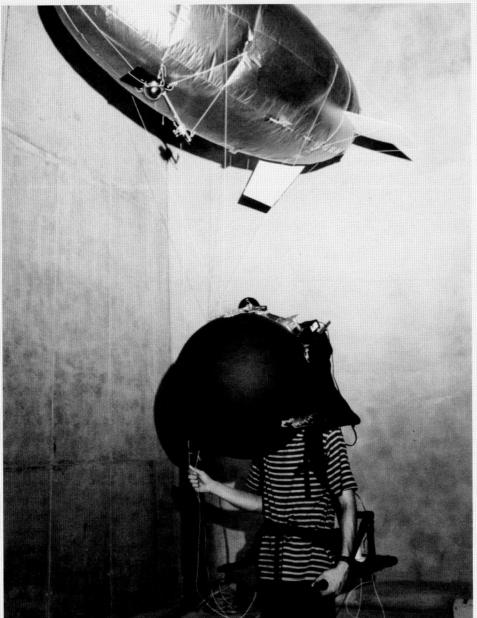

Hiroo Iwata
Floating Eye
2001

*Floating Eye is an interactive installation
that separates a person's vision from
the body. The participant navigates
a floating airship by towing a string.
The airship is equipped with a specialized
camera-head that captures a wide-angle
image. A wearable visual system then
allows the participant to see his/her own
body or the surrounding environment
from a bird's perspective.*

In the history of avant-garde art, there existed programs such as E.A.T. [4]. In recent
years in Japan, there has been an understanding that artists' creative ideas help the
industry to develop new technology or to find new applications. As a result, media
artists are often invited to universities to work with researchers in engineering, on
public grants for projects that bridge art and technology.

Troika: Device art seems based on a different understanding of art in Japan from
the West. How do you think device art can become acceptable in the West? Is it
possible at all? Under what circumstances?

MK: As I said earlier, Japanese media artists are often criticized for their apparently
playful attitude towards technology. But an artwork can be both playful and critical
at the same time. For example, Maywa Denki's [pp. 254–59] works have rich cultural
layers behind their funny representation. Regarding the positive attitude towards
technology, it is important to understand that Japan did not share the nightmare
of the industrial revolution, which so heavily influenced Western culture. Besides,
during nearly 250 years of peace from the 17th to the mid-19th century, the latest
technologies were used for entertainment instead of for warfare or for industry. Of
course, Japan had to quickly catch up with the West after that, but optimism about

[4]
E.A.T. (Experiments in Art and
Technology) was founded in 1966
by engineers Billy Klüver and
Fred Waldhauer and artists Robert
Rauschenberg and Robert Whitman.
The non-profit organization developed
from the experience of '9 Evenings:
Theatre and Engineering'. This event,
which was held in October 1966 in New
York City, brought together 40 engineers
and 10 contemporary artists who
worked together on performances that
incorporated new technology.

Nobumichi Tosa (Maywa Denki) poses
with two of his 'singing machines'.

technology seems to be deeply rooted in Japanese culture. (For example, compare
Fritz Lang's film Metropolis with its Japanese version, an animation written by the
manga master Osamu Tezuka and realized by Katsuhiro Otomo, the director of
Akira.) However, our society has already gone through the modern era, entered the
postmodern era, and now we live in the information age. Artists respond to such changes
in society. It always takes longer for art institutions to accept change, but growing
public acceptance eventually influences the definition of art. Such a transition takes
place especially in fields where the 'public' is involved in supporting the new art form.
Photography and film came through such a process. It's happening with music video
now, and in design as well, I believe. People are accepting the idea that creators can
express their ideas and concepts in commercially available formats. Device art is
a part of such a phenomenon.

Troika: What parallels can you draw between the Japanese device art movement and
the other designers/artists included in this book — Hulger, Science and Sons, Fur,
Schulze and Webb, Aparna Rao?

MK: There are many parallels among these movements including device art, because
they are responding to our contemporary society from different, though non-traditional
angles. Besides movements in art and design, I see important parallels in culture to
share, such as the open-source movement and Creative Commons [5], do-it-yourself,
the 'Make' community [6], among others. We live in the information-based society,
in which digital technologies have changed what 'copy' or 'copyright' or 'publishing'
means, while the industry is dominated by IT giants. How do we secure and develop
our right to use technology creatively? In the field of design, mass-production
technologies have made it possible for the general public to enjoy 'design' in daily
life. It was made possible by designers who collaborated creatively with the industry.
Already in the 19th century Christopher Dresser [7] pioneered such collaboration,
offering functional and refined design for everyday life. Designers today, such as
Naoto Fukasawa [8], collaborate with industry to realize new concepts that engineers

[5]
The Creative Commons is a non-profit
organization devoted to expanding the
range of creative work available for
others legally to build upon and share.
The organization has released several
copyright licences known as Creative
Commons licences, which restrict only
certain rights (or none) of the work.

[6]
Make is a quarterly publication from
O'Reilly Media, which focuses on
DIY projects celebrating technology,
science, and craft with a DIY mindset.
Make is marketed to people who enjoy
'making' things and features complex
projects that can often be completed
with cheap materials, including
household items.

[7]
Christopher Dresser (1834–1904) was
one of the first industrial designers and
pioneered what we now recognize as
the spruce, simple, modern aesthetic.
He embraced modern manufacturing
in the development of furniture,
textiles, ceramics, glass, wallpaper
and metalware and used it to introduce
well-made and efficient products into
the homes of ordinary people. His metal
toast racks are still in production today.

would not imagine. Artists do not have to stand outside society, technology, actual production or reality, even if their ideas can be best realized outside museums and galleries. These movements reflect such ideas.

Troika: How much of device art aims at creating a sustainable income stream for the artist, beyond traditional gallery sales?

MK: We are just finding this out. In most cases, mass production requires involvement of professional production/distribution companies. This means that artists will be paid some kind of licensing fee for each product sold. A popular product will bring the artist a sustainable income. While it is not exactly device art, as it is software, Kazuhiko Hachiya's PostPet [9] is a most successful example, in which an artist proposed a product idea to a company on his own initiative, resulting in a product that has brought considerable income to both the company and himself over the last ten years. It is possible.

Troika: Why do you think technology companies do not produce designer items or hire individual designers as much as furniture companies do?

MK: In the case of furniture, the basic function cannot be changed. Therefore design becomes a means of attracting attention. However, function is the major focus of attention in the case of technology-oriented products. Besides, there is not much freedom for design when realizing function is the matter in hand. In Japan, technology companies hire individual designers to produce cell phones and robots, which is an interesting phenomenon. These are highly technical products in which function seriously matters, but they are also cultural objects. Design is a major issue. So the companies hire outstanding individual designers if they think that they will help attract attention and discover unexpected design possibilities.

[8]
Naoto Fukasawa is a lecturer in the Product Design department at Musashino Art University and Tama Art University in Tokyo. He helped set up IDEO in Japan in 1996 and his designs have won more than 50 design awards in Europe and America.

[9]
PostPet is an email software that was developed by Kazuhiko Hachiya (media artist), Namie Manabe (graphic designer) and Takashi Kohki (programmer) in 1997. Sony Communication Network Corporation handles production, distribution and user support.

INDEX

A

from left to right

B

C

F / G
from left to right

Front
[Sofia Lagerkvist,
Charlotte von der
Lancken, Anna Lindgren,
Katja Sävström]
pp.48, 291

fur
[Volker Morawe,
Tilman Reiff]
pp.158, 292

Michael Golembewski
pp.170, 292

 G / H

Greyworld
[Neil Gavin, Andrew
Shoben, Adriana Paice]
pp.132, 292

Mark Hansen
pp.86, 292

Usman Haque
pp.62, 292

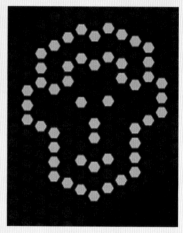

Mark Hauenstein
pp.204, 292

HeHe
[Helen Evans,
Heiko Hansen]
pp.156, 293

Simon Heijdens
pp.58, 293

 H / I

Jeppe Hein
pp.98, 293

Hulger
[Nicolas Roope,
Michael-George Hemus,
Aimee Furnival]
pp.196, 293

Roger Ibars
pp.190, 293

from left to right

Industrial Facility
[Ippei Matsumoto,
Sam Hecht]
pp.202, 295

**The Institute for
Applied Autonomy**
pp.142, 294

Takeshi Ishiguro
pp.42, 294

Natalie Jeremijenko
pp.228, 294

Crispin Jones
pp.242, 294

Sachiko Kodama
pp.122, 276, 294

Onkar Kular
pp.252, 294

Machiko Kusahara
pp.274, 295

Ryota Kuwakubo
pp.210, 295

L

Joris Laarman
pp.22, 295

Jürg Lehni
pp.174, 295

Kok-Chian Leong
pp.248, 295

M/O

P

from left to right

R

R/S

W / Z

from left to right

Matt Webb
pp.192, 301

Philip Worthington
pp.162, 302

Tristan Zimmermann
[Science & Sons]
pp.200, 302

BIOGRAPHIES

Mitch Altman

b. 1956 (Chicago), lives and works in San Francisco. Mitch Altman received Bachelor and Master of Science degrees in Electrical Engineering from the University of Illinois. Altman has been a consultant in electronics and computers for most of his career, although he has been involved in many different projects. He was previously part of the team at the pioneering firm VPL Research, which coined the term 'virtual reality' and created the first virtual reality machines. He founded Cornfield Electronics following his invention of the TV-B-Gone, and has been involved in several community building activities and collaborations with non-profit organizations such as the San Francisco Bicycling Coalition and the Online Policy Group (recycling computers for re-use).

info@TVBGone.com
www.cornfieldelectronics.com

Paola Antonelli

b. 1963 (Milan, Italy), lives and works in New York. Paola Antonelli joined the Museum of Modern Art in February 1994 and is a Curator in the Department of Architecture and Design. Her first exhibition for MoMA was 'Mutant Materials in Contemporary Design' (1995). Several others followed, covering all facets of architecture and design in the contemporary world. The most recent, 'Design and the Elastic Mind' (2008), was devoted to the changes in scale and pace that we experience in our everyday lives and to the fundamental role of design in helping us cope with them. Indeed, her ultimate goal is to make design the best loved, understood and celebrated subject of the 21st century. Among her current projects are a book about foods from all over the world as examples of outstanding design and an attempt to get a Boeing 747 into the collection of the Museum of Modern Art.

Paola_Antonelli@moma.org
www.moma.org

Ron Arad

b. 1951 (Tel Aviv, Israel), lives and works in London. Ron Arad has emerged as one of the most influential designers of our time. In 1981, he co-founded with Caroline Thorman the design and production studio One Off and, in 1989, Ron Arad Associates architecture and design practice. He is currently Professor of Design Products at the Royal College of Art, London. Alongside his limited-edition studio work, he designs for many leading international companies including Kartell, Vitra, Moroso, Fiam, Alessi, Cappellini, iGuzzini and Magis. His many latest architectural projects include: Battersea Power Station, London; Y's (Yohji Yamamoto) flagship store, Tokyo; Maserati Ferrari headquarters showroom in Modena; Hotel Puerta America, Madrid; the living room and family dining room for Sheikh Saud Al-Thani of Qatar; Vallarta Tower, Guadalajara, Mexico; and Selfridges Technology Hall, London.

info@ronarad.com
www.ronarad.com

Auger–Loizeau

James Auger (b. 1970, London) and Jimmy Loizeau (b. 1968, London) combine a range of disciplines, including engineering, fine art and product design, to develop work that aims to question current design ideology. They have been collaborating on projects since October 2000, when they were studying for a Masters in Design Products from the Royal College of Art, from which they graduated in 2001. Auger and Loizeau are currently tutor and research fellow at the RCA and Goldsmiths College respectively. They have won numerous awards, both individually and together, including the Blue Print Award (1999, UK) (Loizeau), the Köln Klopfer (Cologne Thumper) Designer of the Year 2002 (Auger) and the Future Products Award for Audio-Tooth Implant from the Science Museum London in 2002 (Auger and Loizeau).

info@auger-loizeau.com
www.auger-loizeau.com

CREDITS

16   (17) Pandora, all images supplied by
     Swarovski
18   (19) NeON, all images © Richard Brine
20   Crystallize, image © Andrea Ferrari
21   Crystallize, all images © Richard Brine
22   (23) Bone Chaise, photography by Bas Helbers
24   (top left) Bone Chair, render results: Opel
24   (top right) Bone Chair, photography by
     Bas Helbers
25   Bone Chair, photography by Bas Helbers
26   (27, 28, 29) Laser Dresses, Mechanical Dress -
     1940s-1960s, The Morphing Hood Coat, all
     images supplied by Hussein Chalayan Studio
31   Lolita, Team: Ron Arad Associates, Ron Arad
     (principal designer), Yukiko Tango,
     (electronics), Moritz Waldemeyer, Spencer Tsai
     (photography)
32   (33) Lo-Rez-Dolores-Tabula-Rasa, image
     courtesy Dupont, photography by Tom Vack
33   (bottom) image © Troika
34   (top) Lo-Rez-Dolores-Tabula-Rasa, photography
     by Leo Torry
34   (bottom) image © Troika
35   (top) image © Troika
36   Clone Chaise, photography © Peter Mallet
40   (41) Pegasus and the Winged Lion
     character animation by Carlos De Faria,
     a British Airways commission for Terminal 5,
     Heathrow, curated by Artwise, all images ©
     Alex Delfanne/Artwise Curators 2008
41   Oak Seasons, laser etching by Vitrics, 3D
     modelling by Squint Opera, a British Airways
     commission for Terminal 5, Heathrow, curated
     by Artwise, all images © Alex Delfanne/Artwise
     Curators 2008
42   (43) Book of Lights, all images © Artechnica
44   Flight, photography by Sylvain Deleu
45   (top) Attracted to Light, photography by
     Sylvain Deleu
45   (bottom) Flight, photography by John Marshall
46   (47) Flight, photography by Sylvain Deleu
48   (49) Changing Cupboard, photography by
     Ivan Citelli
59   (60, 61) Reed, Tree, Lightweeds, 3, Rising
     Slowly, all images © Simon Heijdens
62   Open Burble, photography by
     Eng Kiat Tan/Haque Design + Research Ltd
64   (65, 66, 67) Battles,
     Brothers, Volume, Triptych, all images ©
     United Visual Artists
67   Triptych, commissioned by onedotzero
68   (69) BIX communicative display skin
     for the Kunsthaus Graz, conception, design,
     project, management and art direction by Jan
     & Tim Edler/realities:united; project

assistance by Juan Ayala Cortes, Carla
Eckhard, Rainer Hartl, Wolfgang Metschan;
software programming by John deKron, Jeremy
Rotsztain, Peter Castine, Ayala Cortes, Carla
Eckhard, Rainer Hartl, Wolfgang Metschan
(68) photography © 2003 by Landesmuseum
Joanneum
(69) photography © 2003 Harry Schiffer, Graz
70   (71) SPOTS Light and Media Installation at
     Potsdamer Platz, Berlin, conception, design
     and planning by realities:united; team: Jan
     Edler, Tim Edler, Malte Niedringhaus, Stefan
     Tietke, Ulrike Brückner, Carla Eckhard, Erik
     Levander, Christoph Wagner, Jan-Philipp
     Wittrin; software development by John Dekron
     and Jeremy Rotsztain, all images © 2005-06
     Bernd Hiepe, Berlin
72   (73) All the Time in the World, manufactured
     by Elumin8, a British Airways commission
     for Terminal 5, Heathrow, curated by Artwise,
     all images © Alex Delfanne/Artwise Curators
     2008
76   (77, 78, 79, 80, 81) Binary Star, Loop System
     Quintet, Palindrome, © the artist, all images
     courtesy the Victoria Miro Gallery
82   (83, 84, 85) Mechanical Mirrors, all
     photographs courtesy of bitforms gallery, New
     York City, and the artist
86   (88) Listening Post, all images by
     David Allison; © Mark Hansen and
     Ben Rubin 2006, all rights reserved
87   (89) Listening Post, all images ©
     Mark Hansen and Ben Rubin 2006,
     all rights reserved
91   Standards and Double Standards, photography
     by Peter Hauck
92   Synaptic Caguamas, photography by
     Antimodular Research
93   Wavefunction, courtesy of the artist;
     programming by Conroy Badger, simulation by
     Gideon May, production by Pierre Fournier,
     David Lemieux, Natalie Bouchard, Boris
     Dempsey, Paul Duchaine, Sandra Badger,
     Guy Bärtschi and Justine Durrett, production
     support by Vitra, photography by Antimodular,
     all photographs courtesy of bitforms gallery,
     New York City, and the artist, photography
     by Antimodular Research
98   Walking Cube, courtesy of Johann König,
     Berlin, photography by Jeppe Hein
99   Moving Neon Cube, courtesy of Johann König,
     Berlin, photography by Holger Hübsch
100 (101) Changing Neon Sculpture, courtesy of
     Johann König, Berlin, photography by Anders
     Berg/Galleri Nicolai Wallner, Copenhagen

102 (103) Robotic Chair, photography by Nichola
     Feldman-Kiss
104 (105, 106)] Ondulation, audio/visual
     composition by Thomas McIntosh, Mikko
     Hynninen and Emmanuel Madan, engineer for
     the digital realm Hans Samuelson,
     construction by Brian Clark, consulting
     Realworld engineer David Ozsvari; Ondulation
     was produced with the financial assistance
     of the Canada Council for the Arts, the
     Daniel Langlois Foundation for Art, Science
     and Technology, le Conseil des arts et des
     lettres du Québec in partnership with the
     Lume Media Centre in Helsinki and the SAT
     (Société des Arts Technologiques) in
     Montreal. Audio and lighting equipment for
     Ondulation is provided in part by Bryston
     Limited and Selecon. All images © Diana
     Shearwood
112 (113) Machine #1.4, photography by
     Colin Davidson
119 (120, 121) Planet Space Rover, Orgamat,
     Drone #6, Solar Kinetic Object #28,
     all photographs courtesy of bitforms gallery,
     New York City, and the artist
127 (128, 129) Tambourin, Circular Structure, Duo,
     all photographs courtesy of bitforms gallery
     New York City, and the artist
132 (133) The Source, all images © Greyworld, all
     rights reserved
134 Counter Void, direction by Maki and
     Associates, coordinated by Shiraishi
     Contemporary Art, Inc., commissioned by TV
     Asahi
138 (139) Cloud, manufactured by Mike Smith
     Studio, a British Airways commission for
     Terminal 5, Heathrow, curated by Artwise
     images © Alex Delfanne/Artwise Curators
     2008
139 (top) Cloud, image © Troika 2008
146 (147, 148, 149) L.A.S.E.R. Tag, images courtesy
     of Graffiti Research Lab
154 SpokePOV, photography by Limor Fried
155 SpokePOV, photography by Selim Korycki
156 Tapis Volant, photography by HeHe 2005
157 Tapis Volant, photography by Ali Taptik 2005
174 (175, 176, 177) Hektor, Jürg Lehni with
     Uli Franke
178 (179) Rita, produced with Bruno Thurnherr and
     Marcel Ackerknecht from Defekt GmbH, linear
     bearings and brushless DC motors provided by
     Festo Sweden, supported by Sitemapping.ch and
     the Swiss Federal Office of Culture
186 (187, 188, 189) Modified Toys, all images ©
     warmcircuit.com
190 Phaser Shoots Casio © Roger Ibars 2005
191 (top right) Nintendo Guns Shoot Philips
     © Roger Ibars 2003, acquired by private
     collection (Belgium)
191 (top left) Atari Controls Philips © Roger
     Ibars 2005
191 (bottom) Miami Vice © Roger Ibars 2005,
     acquired by Indri Tulusan
197 P*PHONE, photography by Violetta Boxill
200 (201) Phonofone II, photography by Kris
     Belchevski 2007
211 (top right) VideoBulb, image © Yoshimoto
     Kogyo Co. Ltd, Maywa Denki, Ryota Kuwakubo
222 ACCESS, Softopia Center, Ogaki, Gifu,
     Japan, 2002, photography by Arnauld Pilpré
223 ACCESS, Ars Electronica, Linz,
     Austria, 2003, photography by Marie Sester
227 Bra Removal Trainer, commissioned by
     Alexandra Midal for the exhibition 'Tomorrow
     Now' at the MUDAM, Luxembourg, photography by
     Andres Lejona
235 (236, 237) Technological Dream Series: No. 1,
     Robots, commissioned by z33; thanks to Per
     Tingleff, Graeme Findley, Ben Legg, James
     Auger, Simon Denzel, Bahbak Hashemi-Nehzad,
     Wakana and Mo
238 (239) Do You Want to Replace the Existing
     'Normal'?, thanks to the Arts Council, London;
     David Austen, Berry Place; James Chappell,

     Berry Place; Nick Williamson (Exploder);
     Chris Hand (Statistical Clock); David Muth
     (Sex Addiction); Erick Kearney (Risk Watch);
     David England (Exploder); Graeme Findlay;
     Alice Wang; Anya
240 (bottom) Uncle Phone, photography
     by Aparna Rao
241 (top) 22 Pop, photography by
     Ivan Gasparini
242 Mr Jones Watches, design lead and electronic
     prototyping by Crispin Jones, design
     collaborator and prototyper Anton Schubert,
     design collaborator and graphic design Ross
     Cooper, design collaborator Graham Pullin,
     photography by Andrew Powell
243 (top) Katazukue, image © Crispin Jones 2007
243 (bottom) ZXZX, image © Crispin Jones 2007
253 Hari & Parker Commissioned by the Science
     Museum, London for 'The Science of Spying'
     exhibition, 2007
254 (256, 257, 258, 259) all images ©
     Yoshimoto Kogyo Co. Ltd/Maywa Denki,
     photography by Jun Mitsuhashi
260 (261) Electroprobe, 'Shit! I Forgot the iPod!',
     all images © Troika, all rights reserved
271 Not Made by Hand Not Made in China,
     photography by Tom Vack 2000
281 Anthony Dunne, photography by Bill Moggridge
281 portrait Limor Fried, photo by
     Jacob Appelbaum
285 Fiona Raby, photography by Bill Moggridge